GROWTH
TOWARD FREEDOM

GROWTH
TOWARD FREEDOM

A Challenge for Campus and Community

BY

WILLIAM W. BIDDLE

WITH THE COLLABORATION OF

LOUREIDE J. BIDDLE

HARPER & BROTHERS   PUBLISHERS   NEW YORK

Library of Congress catalog card number: 56–9086

TO

Bruce and Ellen
Kathie and Bob

Contents

Contents

Preface

In education men have evolved an instrument for the shaping of the future, for the reshaping of themselves. Why do free men fail to use it boldly?

An age of unprecedented change is upon us. The times inspire both fear and hope, but fear is the predominating mood. The times challenge the best wisdom and ethical sensitiveness accumulated from the past. They challenge the best of flexible intelligence to guide the future. They call upon the disciplined wisdom of educators to guide progress. Why is education not utilized more actively to solve the great practical problems men must face? Because so few people look upon it as something primarily useful.

The word "education" can call up at least two pictures. One deals with institutions. The other is concerned with processes. The institutions were set up to carry on the processes. But organizational structure takes on a life of its own, irrespective of the purpose it was meant to serve. As a system of education becomes more magnificent, it collects admiration and support for being, not for contributing. Education as process emphasizes growth. Its worth is more likely to be measured by what it does—to people. The more elaborate the institutions the better equipped are they to serve, if they will. The two concepts are not incompatible as long as the basic purpose— service to people—is kept in mind.

In an age of fearful uncertainty, socially responsible educators will seek to make their knowledge and skill available to restless humanity-on-the-march. There is no more fundamental obligation for them to accept than the encouragement of human development toward freedom. There certainly are means for contributing to self-development other than those we have proposed. There are ways of bringing education to bear upon the pressing problems of men, other than adoption of a broadly-defined fundamental education by higher education. Colleges and universities hold no monopoly of teaching. And the authors of this book hold no monopoly of ideas for bringing education to bear upon the problems of humanity in flux.

Despite these disclaimers, two statements seem justified. First, any educational effort to help men find their way that does not utilize the facilities of higher education will fall tragically short of meeting the need. Second, any such effort should give serious heed to the philosophy of inspiring self-help which this book attempts to state and illustrate.

Educators who continue with the even tenor of their ways, who have nothing to offer to struggling humanity, have thrown their weight on the side of confusion and disorder, by default. The wisdom, the hope, the self-discipline to grow toward responsible freedom—these are the keys to a future tolerable to humanity. Is there a more delicate and difficult task, a higher challenge to come to higher education?

WILLIAM W. BIDDLE
LOUREIDE J. BIDDLE

I dare to affirm the belief that this will be called the century in which man abolished war, established economic justice, and realized racial brotherhood.

Trotsky insisted that the system that produces goods most efficiently will win. What he did not realize was that while man does need commodity, he likewise needs community. It is much more likely that the system that can develop community will survive when in competition with a system that produces commodity without community.

—Bishop G. Bromley Oxnam, speaking before the National Convocation of Methodist Youth at Purdue University, August 24, 1955.

GROWTH
TOWARD FREEDOM

Chapter I

FREEDOM'S STRONGEST WEAPON

Education is the most potent weapon that free men have for defense of freedom. Most people endorse this statement during periods of calm. They regard it as inappropriate for the turbulent times of fear. Thus they reject the one method of dealing with people that would give direction and completion to all other defenses of freedom. In the contemporary era of change, failure to utilize this instrument may bring an end to the liberties free men already possess. They had best use education with vigor; the disadvantaged majority of humanity now demands the privileges which have been denied them for ages. Are they moving toward the freedom of active responsibility or toward enslavement made palatable by the facile promises of easily-gained privilege?

Freedom cannot remain an exclusive possession of the technically advanced West. It must increase or contract. It must become available to all or it will become less available to the fortunate few who know it. Military events, economic aid, enlightened diplomacy, can expedite freedom. But it can spread with permanence only as a result of changes in people.

The Gap of Privilege Will Close

There is a new fact in human history; the majority who have labored in hopeless want need do so no longer. The "have-nots" see the possibility of enjoying the luxuries of the "haves." The enormous productivity made possible by scientific advances and industrialization have made a materially-privileged status available to a majority for the first time, but only within those nations that have dared to experiment with freedom. The United States represents the vanguard of this unprecedented avdvance toward plenty.

1

In this country the level of living for the now privileged majority constantly rises. The gap of privilege widens not because those at the bottom sink lower—they cannot do so and survive. It widens because those at the top rise to heights that make difficult communication with, or understanding of, their brothers who remain at age-old levels of misery.

Most of the human race still lives in the midst of endemic despair. Fully 50 per cent of the world's population is perpetually hungry. Between 50 and 65 per cent is illiterate, unable to receive communication except by word of mouth. In the United States alone ten million persons are "functionally illiterate" (schooling no higher than fifth grade). Are comfortable Americans aware of the gulf that separates them from the majority of their fellows? While they accept railroads and highways and trucks and automobiles as normal, do they realize that available food cannot be carried to many parts of the world for lack of transportation facilities? While they worry about surpluses and limits on production, do they know that a material minimum for decent living is unknown to whole populations? For the bulk of humanity neither overweight nor overproduction are problems.

The gap of privilege will close. The disadvantaged many will no longer accept a hopeless fate with resignation. If those at the top will not help them to rise, they will seize the material blessings they covet, thereby reducing the wealthier few toward their own level. Or they may fight for the goods they lack without growing toward the freedom that produced them. Twentieth-century productivity will force a closing of the gap, either by supplying the articles that bless or the weapons that destroy. In potential, poverty is out of date. So are illiteracy and ignorance, as well as many diseases that have plagued men.[1] Are privileged Americans aware of the revolutionary possibilities inherent in this potential?

---

[1] Those who make optimistic statements must take into consideration two forces that work in opposition to each other: First, the fabulous productivity made possible by applied science and industrial "know-how." Second, the explosive population increase that usually follows increase in supply of food and health services. Many fear that the second will cancel out the first. Whether such a dismal prospect faces the human race will not be known until human beings make use of productive skill, and develop a willingness to experiment with improvement on worldwide scale. Then scientific thinking will have to be applied to problems of population increase as well as to problems of production. Neither shortage of goods nor surplus of people lie beyond the intelligence of men, if that intelligence can be stirred to operate responsibly among all men. Men cannot hope to gain

Not all citizens of the United States are wealthy, but the nation is unique in having brought a high and rising standard of living to a majority within its borders. Such success imposes a unique obligation. Those who possess privilege can be sure of their future only as they succeed in helping the less fortunate up toward their own standard of living and toward a self-achieved freedom.

Poverty and attendant evils will never be conquered permanently by gift from the "haves" to the "have-nots." The important end-to-be-sought is not possession of food or shelter or medical services, but the achievement of the ability to produce these as needed. Help that supplies people's needs merely tends to enslave; help that inspires self-productive initiative tends to free. In the long run, the under-privileged must rise to a higher status by their own efforts. But they will and must take a shorter road to privilege than the "haves" of industrial nations have traveled. With wise and patient encouragement most of them can move into the twentieth century before it has run its course. The threatening times call for great speed of human change. They call also for the utmost of educational skill to inspire self-help that produces results and yet does not curtail the growth of initiative.

American efforts to close the gap of privilege should not be turned primarily toward the shipping of supplies to those in need. Despite its tremendous productivity this country cannot feed and clothe the whole human race. The "have-nots" must and can produce for themselves. The United States must become not the world supplier of goods but the world supplier of ideas and encouragement. Contrary to the assumptions of most opponents of foreign aid, the money should be spent for education to stir self-help, not for goods to be distributed.

The United States also represents the most extensive system of education in the world. Then the nation should contain a large number of men and women capable of contributing to the growth of their fellows. But any and every kind of education will not serve the cause of freedom. In fact, modern dictators have found schools and teachers indispensable aids to slavery. Teaching is a tool that can be used

---

the benefits that arise from applying rational scientific thinking to one area of life and withhold it from other areas. If they attempt to do so, the gains in one area will be canceled by dislocations arising from others.

according to the purposes of the user. Without calling in question any traditional efforts of instruction, it must be pointed out that the desperation of man's need for growth demands a fresh examination of the usefulness of the American instructional machinery. Some educators have been feeling their way toward a restatement of the purposes and methods which are basic to mankind's contemporary need in a type of effort coming to be known as fundamental education.

WHAT IS FUNDAMENTAL?

As thoughtful people have become aware of the explosive possibilities of a tragically underdeveloped majority in the world, they have begun to seek ways to reduce the contrast between the privileged few and the resentful many. There is need among the underprivileged for material things, technical equipment, capital. But there is need also for educational processes, skills to handle new equipment, knowledge and equipment that will allow communication with the rest of the human race, changes in points of view, growth toward initiative and responsibility. Since the end of the second World War there have been many attempts to meet this enormous and multi-faceted educational need, carried on by a variety of agencies, governmental and private, under a variety of names, and with many functions and emphases.

The variety is bewildering. In the early days some experts referred to their job as *Mass Education*. The mass approach was dictated both by awareness of the needy multitudes and by new instruments of communication. It is still necessary, but insufficient. Then some claimed the activity as a branch of *Adult Education*. This designation is also too limited, since childhood learning is often part of the process. Gandhi talked of *Social Education*. Then the term *Basic Education* has been used. *Fundamental Education* as a title was first proposed by UNESCO, although many others have borrowed it since. Recently the specialty known as *Community Development* has come into common acceptance, sometimes used as synonymous with fundamental education. It is certainly an essential part, but not the whole. There is now an emerging general agreement upon the term *Fundamental Education* as the broadest, all-inclusive title for the task of stimulating self-help among underdeveloped people.

Consider, however, some of the confusions on content and scope of activity:

An announcement of a project in fundamental education training defines it as "basic education for illiterates to enable them to raise their standard of living." [2]

A pamphlet published by UNESCO describes the purpose of fundamental education: "to help people develop what is best in their own culture" and "to obtain the active participation of the people themselves in shaping their own future." [3]

Since this type of education has been carried on mainly by the United Nations, the American State Department, foreign mission organizations, and other agencies of international outreach, there has been a general assumption that it deals mainly or exclusively with the "backward" people in foreign lands. In contrast, the Board for Fundamental Education, chartered by the United States Congress in 1954, carries on activity among underdeveloped peoples in rural and urban setting, entirely within the United States.[4] The scope of activity may be concentrated upon preparation of material for mass distribution on such specific topics as teaching of reading to illiterates, hygiene and sanitation, farm methods, and hand industries.

The function may sometimes be broadened in such statements as: "Areas where a high proportion of the people are illiterate are the main field for fundamental education. The skills of reading, writing, and counting are not, however, an end in themselves. Rather, they are the essential means to the achievement of a fuller and more creative life." [5]

On the other hand, the method passes far beyond preparation of mass materials in such a statement as "Fundamental education is concerned with the community as a whole, and should lead to action. The methods must therefore be chosen with this end in view: to help people help themselves." [6]

An Evolving Definition

Concepts of fundamental education have gone through several

[2] U. S. State Dept., Jan. 7, 1955.
[3] *Fundamental Education, Description and programme*, No. 1 (Paris: UNESCO, 1947), p. 16.
[4] Board for Fundamental Education, 156 Fifth Ave., New York 10, N. Y.
[5] UNESCO, *op. cit.*, p. 15.
[6] *Ibid.*, p. 12.

sequences of emphasis. One is purpose—from literacy for adults, to technical skills in agriculture and industry, to knowledges for decent living, to skills in working together, to the encouragement of self-help. Another sequence of change moves from concentration upon underdeveloped foreigners, to consideration of the underprivileged at home, to inclusion of any people who could be developed further.

If an education be fundamental, it is fundamental to whom, to what? If its purpose be to bring underdeveloped people up to "our" level, then it is arrogant and may create resistance among those to whom it is addressed. If its purpose be to increase the autonomy of underdeveloped people and their ability to solve their problems democratically, intelligently, and with good will, then it can serve a purpose which is fundamental to the learner as well as to the educator. A satisfactory definition will attempt to pull together various trends in a changing activity, but in such a way as to enhance the dignity of the learner. Among the best comprehensive statements is the following:

Fundamental education is that kind of minimum and general education which aims to help children and adults who do not have the advantages of formal education to understand the problems of their immediate environment and their rights and duties as citizens and individuals, and to participate more effectively in the economic and social progress of their community.

It is "fundamental" in the same sense that it gives the minimum knowledge and skills which are an essential condition for attaining an adequate standard of living. It is prerequisite to the full effectiveness of work in health, agriculture, and similar skilled services.

It is general in the sense that this knowledge and these skills are not imparted for their own sake only. It uses active methods, it focuses interest on practical problems in the environment, and in this way it seeks to develop both individual and social life.

It is concerned with children for whom there is no adequate system of primary schooling and with adults deprived of educational opportunities; it utilizes all suitable media for their development through individual effort and through community life.

Fundamental education must awaken a consciousness of human dignity and develop a sense of the cultural and moral solidarity of mankind.[7]

[7] Lionel Elvin, "What Fundamental Education Is" in *The Year Book of Education 1954*, p. 581.

To the extent that this definition is tied to people, their development, their dignity, their moral solidarity, it is adequate. To the extent that it is tied to those who have been denied formal schooling or limited to specific skills, it falls short. The most important educational task is the stimulation of growth toward freedom in all men, wherever they are, on a worldwide scale. *That education is fundamental which encourages people to develop themselves by solving problems in their own way, at their own pace, according to methods and objectives they have selected in consultation with trusted friends. It is fundamental because it is directed toward gaining for men some control over their own destiny.*

Such a definition is in line with the best thinking of leaders in the work of fundamental education, though many have been too busy to seek out the theoretical implications of their changing thinking. Three quotations from UNESCO sources will make clear the broadening understanding of that which is fundamental.

Fundamental education is a world issue, not just a programme, to help the men and women of all countries to live fuller and happier lives, to achieve the social and economic progress which will enable them to take their place in the modern world and to live together in peace.[8]

Fundamental education should aim at promoting understanding and sympathy between peoples not only of different races or tribes, but also of different religious persuasions.[9]

The task of Fundamental Education is to cover the whole of living. In addition, it is to teach not only new ways, but the need and incentive for new ways.[10]

When an educational movement becomes a world issue, a potential world saver, it should become a matter of concern to thoughtful leaders of every nation. Is there an instrument here by which men and women can learn to lift themselves out of the doldrums of frustration and quiet despair? Is there a means of help which can inspire self-help and self-development? If there is, then educators of every kind had best reexamine their own responsibilities lest they be missing the most important opportunity which an age of challenge and crisis can offer.

[8] UNESCO, *op. cit.*, pp. 81–82.
[9] UNESCO, *op. cit.*, p. 48.
[10] Margaret Mead, ed., *Culture Patterns and Technical Change* (Paris: UNESCO, 1953), pp. 269–70.

UNDERPRIVILEGED AND UNDERDEVELOPED

Though fundamental education is concerned with stimulating self-development in learners, teachers are not eliminated. Growth toward freedom cannot be counted upon to occur spontaneously, nor in appropriate form, nor fast enough, to meet the needs of the times. The educator is necessary but he will frequently find himself under pressure to change his ways.

Such teaching always involves a mixing of two or more civilizations, cultures, economic levels, or levels of sophistication within a culture. There is almost always an implication of superiority and inferiority: the teacher looks upon the background that produced him as more meritorious or advanced. Out of such mixing can come conflict and violence; out of unskillful teaching can come misunderstanding and suspicion. In the modern world of rapid travel and social fluidity, the mixing cannot be stopped. The educator who seeks fundamental objectives uses situations of contrasting cultures to stimulate growth of understanding, confidence, and initiative in learners. His skill is put to the test in inspiring people less privileged than he to improve in their own way, with the stimulation of "outside" wisdom.

Should the industrial peoples of western civilization seek to carry their technical skills, ways of life, values (and accompanying problems) to the underdeveloped peoples of earth? Said a spokesman for the U. S. Foreign Operation's Administration (later the International Cooperation Administration):

The theory on which we work, so far as Technical Cooperation is concerned, is based on our faith that we, in the advanced countries, have learned how to attack certain problems; that certain other countries have not learned this; and that the best way to help them is to share our knowledge and our techniques with them. Thus the main task is to teach these other people; to help them develop the experts they need.[11]

Says a representative of an "underdeveloped" people (India): Unfortunately, however, the policy of spreading Western thought and science, though conceived in charity, was inspired by arrogance born of conquest.[12]

[11] William F. Russell, "Education, Happiness and Safety," *Teachers College Record*, Feb. 1955, p. 246.
[12] D. K. Hingorani, "Higher Education in India: Recent Developments," *Higher Education*, Feb. 1955, p. 78.

The representatives of Western Civilization make a bad start once they announce that they come from an "advanced" country. Their usefulness as fundamental educators turns upon their interpretation of the word "share." Are they willing to examine the wisdom of the peoples they would help? Are the experts to be trained for self-help merely to parrot the learning of the teachers or are they to work out a new synthesis that embodies some of the tradition of the learners?

Would the human race be brought closer to solution of its problems if all underdeveloped peoples throughout the world were brought "up" to "our" level? When men industrialize, mechanize, and increase their standard of material possession, are they better off? As greater productivity is brought to "less advanced" peoples, will there be also the increase in delinquency, broken families, and disintegrated communities that have been found in the "developed" sections of the industrial West? The attempt to bring "backward" peoples "up" to "our advanced" standards suggests that there is but one road of proper development for men, the one that "we" have followed, the one which has brought in profusion both frightening problems and material goods.

Some thinkers wonder if we might not bring to underdeveloped nations the blessings of Western Civilization without the curses; the productivity, the sanitation and health, the democratic methods, the religious values. Industrialization and mechanization are so new, even to those nations that have known them longest, that no man can separate the good from the bad with certainty. It may be also that if the development of any other nation moves toward goals presented complete by a Westerner who lacks skill, the blessings and curses will come together in an unbreakable "package." The American educator who operates in foreign lands is often prone to exaggerate the achievements of his homeland as a pattern. He might be less self-assured if he had more experience with the underdeveloped folk of his own land. He might even come to see the wisdom of encouraging other nations to pursue some goals of development other than those he accepts. Perhaps other nations might select out the best of an industrial society to be combined with their own traditions. The fundamental educator will not encourage such a new synthesis unless he is willing to accept the citizen of another nation as a person with much to offer.

No nation can offer itself as a perfect pattern for imitation. The educator needs to do something about injustice and ill-treatment at home if he is not to appear insincere to foreigners. The approach and philosophy he uses abroad are applicable to his own domestic disadvantaged. Dare he assume that his disadvantaged fellow citizens will follow the objectives in development that he has accepted out of his probable middle-class background? He must make clear his respect for their dignity also. He will be a genuine fundamental educator when he assumes that even the "lesser" folk at home may have much to contribute to solutions of their own and the world's problems.

The difficulty connected with the use of the word "underprivileged" can be met by limiting its use to some objective statistical measure. Indexes of per capita income offered by economists provide a material basis for comparison of privilege. Nutritionists can report on food consumption, number of calories per day, proportion of protein, availability of vitamins. Public health experts can tell of the incidence of diseases and officers of education the percentage of illiteracy or average amount of formal education. For each measure it is possible to obtain comparative figures and to agree upon some level of privilege below which no civilized nation should be allowed to fall. As used in this book, privilege will refer to these objective (and material) measures. The subtle personal and religious values are important but cannot be included in any discussion that implies judgment on the worth of people.

The difficulty connected with the use of the word "underdeveloped" can also be overcome by admitting the obvious truth that everyone on earth is underdeveloped. There are no fully developed nations to be exhibited as models. Every people is in process of development and probably always will be. There is no single goal or pattern toward which all should move. Variety in objectives is to be welcomed rather than feared as long as there is free exchange of points of view, as long as the advocates of one concept of development do not seek to impose their views upon all others. Even the clearly privileged are capable of further development. Indeed, the most privileged peoples of a privileged nation like the United States are often those who stand in greatest need of development toward social responsibility and the skills of working together. Those who live at a lower standard of living are often more flexible because they are freer to admit that there is something wrong and that they are in need of development.

Who are the learners upon whom the fundamental educator should concentrate attention? Not just foreigners, not just illiterates, not just those who are underprivileged in ways which make them pitiable or picturesque. All human beings lie within the scope of fundamental education, all human beings in process of self-directed development toward more adequate living in the modern world, toward the ability to solve their problems in good will, together. At any given time, for practical reasons, the effort must be concentrated upon some selected limited segment of people. But never should the need for development of all humanity be forgotten, lest the fundamental contribution to growth of freedom be forgotten.

"The Fundamentals"

Certain basic elements must be found in all fundamental education—elements necessary to variety and freedom. But no rigid listing of basic emphases or learnings can be adopted, because self-development calls for a participation in choosing on the part of learners. The educator can recommend that which seems, to him, to point toward the greater freedom of self-choosing. The learner must be free to accept or reject or modify that which would enhance his freedom.

Fundamental educators carry over from their experience with formal schooling certain unfortunate habits and attitudes. Among these is a naïve use of the term "the fundamentals." In school practice this term refers to reading, writing, and arithmetic and possibly some other subject-matters-for-instruction. By analogy, there should be "fundamentals" for those who have missed formal schooling; again reading, writing, and arithmetic and some other prescribed subject-matters. The analogy, of course, is questionable, but more serious is the fact that both uses refer to tools rather than to development of people as fundamental. Perhaps all would agree that growth of responsible personalities is the basic aim of all education. The difficulties arise when pursuit of subject-matter tools obscures the basic purpose. Acquisition of skills and knowledges is defended as fundamental to freedom, but too great an admiration for the tools can impede progress toward the goal they were meant to serve. It is more important to offer the experience of responsible choosing, than to enforce any instruction upon learners.

Keeping in mind the fundamental purpose of growth toward freedom, there are certain tool learnings necessary to emergence into the privileges of the twentieth century. As a preliminary, most educators and learners would agree upon the following minimal list of essentials:

Literacy, the ability to read and write (the learner's own language at least), to count, and to carry on minor arithmetic operations.

Familiarity with certain health and sanitation practices that become acceptable within a community. (When the practice becomes specific, there is often difficulty caused by violation of religious belief and social custom.)

Closely related is education for better nutrition. (This matter is also frequently made difficult by local custom, but also by low economic income and tenaciously-held farming practices.)

Some development pointed toward improved economic standards. (This statement is extremely broad; it covers a multitude of activities, agricultural and industrial. There is therefore enormous room for difference of opinion. It is when new ways of making a living are brought in that many of the evils of Western Society begin to intrude.)

An increase of local ability to work together in village or community. (All the above, though basic to freedom, will not produce freedom unless a people have the local experience of meeting together, of talking, planning and choosing together, of acting together. The nation-wide and world-wide democracy, that will allow variety, begins on the local scene. The encouragement of local autonomy will allow for variety even in forms of democracy.)

The agreement on fundamental elements diminishes as one moves down the list from first to last. The specific form which all the emphases may take will call for vigorous differences of opinion. The last item, ability to work together, has come to be recognized only belatedly. And there are still many who, because of a love for mass education, give this item only slight recognition. But if the self-moving responsibility of democracy (perhaps differently interpreted for different peoples) is important, then the last item is fundamental.

FREEDOM, A COLLECTIVE ACHIEVEMENT

The United States would prove a more effective leader for the free world if more of its citizens understood the nature of freedom. Many influential voices talk as though the inheritors of a precious tradition need only give allegiance to the documents and attitudes of the past and maintain military strength against external enemies. They have forgotten that eternal vigilance is the price of liberty.

Freedom is never a gift. It is an achievement of laborious effort in every generation, among every people. The benefit to individual growth comes not in enjoying a condition but in striving for an ideal. There are times when it must be defended against enemies, external and internal, but victory does not guarantee its triumph. The triumph comes only in the changed lives of citizens as they move toward responsible autonomy.

Freedom is thus not exportable. The idea, the hope, the encouragement: these are exportable. The educational processes that should support the striving can be carried to a distant people to aid their progress toward the responsibility of self-choosing. Such educational efforts are more convincing to foreigners if it is apparent that companion efforts are addressed also to citizens at home, since effective liberty must forever remain an ideal of striving for all men.

An additional disturbing thought intrudes upon man's age-long search for freedom; is the immense productivity made possible by technical advance to be purchased by loss of individual autonomy? Even though nations gain independence from imperialism, do they surrender local and citizen initiative to the complexities of industry and decision-making over which individuals have no control?

Frustrated Individual—Amorphous Mass

The reduction of individuals to a faceless mass in modern dictatorships is easy to describe and to deplore. But such a reduction is to be found in other nations and social systems as well. The tendency grows, in its own form, within the United States. And former colonialisms-become-nations cannot hope to escape the problem by becoming anti-communist or anti-fascist. The rediscovery of the individual for modern times will not be made by opposing dictatorial theories of government or by enthusiastically accepting nationalism or technical productivity. Americans can help all men find the answer for themselves by utilizing their tradition of freedom in an education that matures men toward responsible self-choosing.

The American form of conformity has been created partly by the development of mass communication. The unit of living lost its local flavor and gradually became identified with the area of coverage of the instrument of communication, whether newspaper or magazine or radio or television. These devices have tended to produce mass applause for the few who reach the top. Large scale distribution of news, mass entertainment, broadcast religious services, the admiration for the success story, the belief that bigger and better are synonymous—these all contribute to the diminution of the individual in his own and in his neighbor's eyes. But more important, the individual, a separately operating entity (by naïve democratic definition) loses his autonomy, his conviction that he has any power to affect the apparently uncontrollable course of events. He is less a person in his own right, with some power of decision. He is instead a member of a crowd, able to listen, to complain, or to applaud, and to vote *en masse* once every four years.

The conformity to social pressure that David Riesman has found in American life [13] is an expression of the loss of self-direction which countless individuals feel. Their uniqueness as separate personalities is dimmed because they have no place where their opinions might make a difference, where their voices might be raised to affect the policies and events that control their lives. Since they are convinced that they can do nothing to reshape their fate, the greatest virtue is conformity.

An Intermediary Group

Unique individualism does not come from ruthless competitive struggle that allows one man to beat down all rivals. Individual personality develops in mutual interaction with other personalities. Uniqueness of personality is available to the many only as a result of experience with groups intermediary between the impotent lone individual and the conforming crowd. The problem for the fundamental educator is to find and utilize the groups that can give an experience of self-direction to individuals. Such groups are frequently found to be in existence among underprivileged peoples, though usually they are not utilized for educational purposes. Among privileged peoples, such groups have been disintegrating during the period of industrial progress. They must be recreated or some substitute developed, if individuals are to be encouraged to develop toward freedom.

Historically these intermediary groups have been known as com-

[13] David Riesman, *The Lonely Crowd* (New Haven, Conn.: Yale University Press, 1950).

munities. Among preindustrial people the word may refer to tribes, villages, crossroad settlements, or to country neighborhood groupings with geographic unity. In the cities and suburbs of a technical age, the experience of community is much more difficult to discover or to create. Can it be found or encouraged in a small city, in a block or district, or even in a ghetto or neighborhood of a large city? Educators must search for an answer to this question. In modern life, man's need for experience of community is not easily met.

In searching for a group experience which will reestablish importance and autonomy for individuals, the fundamental educator will be aware of certain criteria for selection: First, the group must be small enough to give a place of recognition to each individual. Each person must have a chance to be heard, to contribute to thinking and to deciding together (even though his recommendations be rejected), to participate in joint action. Second, the group must be large enough to have some collective strength. Whereas the individual alone frequently feels powerless, in company with others he comes to realize that he need not remain a helpless victim; he can become an influencer of events. Third, the group should aspire to be all-inclusive. It should, if possible, include all social classes, races, religions, factions, and points of view which are locally represented.

The fundamental educator should realize that there are two yearnings to be found among underprivileged peoples beyond the desire for creature comforts. These are individual recognition for themselves, and community with other men. These people often fail to realize that the two quests are achieved together. Apart from experience of community, individuality is an abstraction. Apart from strong individuals, community can become a monster enforcing conformity. Experience that will keep the two social yearnings in balance can be found in the local intermediary groups that give recognition to differing individuals, but move on to the real achievement of action together. The fundamental educator will recognize that local community groupings represent his most important operational instruments. They are his "classroom" in which he helps people develop toward a functioning freedom.

All mankind faces the problem of keeping a balance between the separateness of individuality and the pressure toward mass sameness. The individual can find himself in the small community group because others give him recognition. He can begin to gain a sense of self-direction when he has contributed to a collective action which he was able to influence. Local community organization is the social instrument that makes democratic choice possible.

Local community as the means of choosing is but the first step in achievement. Experience of community should not stop there. Longing for individual importance and community with all men can be approximated only as local intermediary group experience becomes the pattern for expanding concepts of community. Individuals who have gained some self-direction with neighbors become stronger and are then able to participate in widening circles of collective thought and action. Though the achievement of the idea starts with a local geographic experience, it can be extended to all the relationships of men, even to those in distant parts of the world.

Worldwide sense of community, brotherhood with all men, the responsibilities of intelligent citizenship—none of these is completely dependent upon first experience with local geographic community. There are those who approach these ends directly in high-level study or discussion, but they represent an intellectual and unusually-motivated minority. Even so, some of these few high-minded need to learn how to adjust to neighbors they can see, as a supplement to loving the brother who lives on the other side of the world. For the majority of men, however, the experience of community begins at home. There the pattern of cooperative brotherhood despite difference is set in human habit. There interest in affairs beyond selfish special interest begins. There the power which Guizot called "the energy of local liberty" is released to help men grow in responsible stature.

The Community Development Approach

In the jargon of fundamental education there is place, for "The Village Approach." In the jargon of adult education as addressed to citizens of the technical West, there is place for "Community Development." Each term refers to a narrow specialty within supposed broader classifications of educational effort. Both are good terms. Their use is to be criticized only when narrowly conceived. If there be a desire to use educational methods to help men grow toward freedom, then the community approach is fundamental. It becomes a focal point around which many specialties of education should be organized.

The first difficulty of a too-narrow concept of community development lies in the tendency to think of it as one specialty among many. The tendency is strong because there are certain skills and items of information a good community developer should possess. But man's need is so great for intermediary group experience that educational processes should not be limited to a series of specific techniques.

The second difficulty lies in limiting use of the word "community" to incorporated villages or cities or to other specifically located accumulations of human beings. Community as instrument for democratic choosing may be found in a number of other social associations.

A third difficulty lies in being satisfied with community achievement at the local level. The significance that lies beyond in changed lives of people and in the spread of an idea to the world scene must ever beckon on the citizen and the educator. Community developers should be encouraged to dream beyond the confines of the immediate task. Community development (flexibly interpreted) is basic to fundamental education (broadly defined).

Numerous specialties of teaching have been added to the repertoire of orthodox fundamental educators over the years. Often these have been added without plan. The acceptance of community development as the basic focus for fundamental education provides a means for building a philosophic purpose that will organize much of present-day educational confusion. Community becomes the focus, not only because better communities are good in themselves but because they are the educational instruments for helping men to gain self-directing responsibility as the condition of freedom.

There are many areas of living in which men can learn to exercise freedom. The area in which growth is most desperately needed is that of citizenship, the field of cooperation together for the common good.

Community is the place where mature adults can begin to regain the power of decision over their own future; where concepts of self-help begin to have meaning in experience; where personal liberty begins to take on reality in voluntary cooperative action together; where any education that is fundamental reaches its focus. There education can concentrate upon community development in order to produce responsible personalities that can live adequately in the modern world.

The Educational Challenge of the Age

The next great forward step is the utilization of communities as educative instruments. The great challenge of the age is the production of men and women committed to an ethical freedom, in the United States, all over the world. Community development and fundamental education interpenetrate. The first requires the second. The latter comes to focus in the former.

What educational institution takes up this challenge? Any that propose to do so had best proceed with self-examining thought, for a broadly-conceived fundamental education must go beyond the present orthodoxies.

An adequate fundamental education directed toward the development of twentieth-century citizens is one which:

Is more concerned with development of free, self-moving, ethical personalities than with learning of any specific subject-matter.

Is activity-centered, rather than centered in classes or courses to be "taken."

Is learner-directed, as much as or more than teacher-directed.

Is conceived in kindly friendship to help people discover the best in themselves, rather than in discipline to force them into some pre-chosen patterns of excellence.

Is a matter of group learning, more than of competitive personal rivalry for marks or grades or approval.

Allows for great variation from one group to another and among individuals within a group, rather than holding all people up to one standard of progress.

Makes learning incidental to problem-solving for action, rather than presenting wisdom in support of scholarship or culture or research, even though these all be desirable objectives to the educator.

Puts the stress upon next steps, more than upon identification of correct theory, even though theoretical thinking must not be neglected.

Seeks to build a hope in people based upon their tested confidence in each other to achieve great things together, more than a hope that rests upon experts or generous givers or even upon wise educators.

Seeks to develop an autonomy of freedom for everyone, more than an autonomy of success for a favored few.

Seeks to help people discover the basic principles of democracy (a theoretical concept) in their own lives, more than seeking a lip endorsement of the democratic principles the educator draws to their attention.

The logical place to center fundamental education through community development is in American universities and colleges. These are the institutions that have the trained personnel, the resources, and the prestige to meet the challenge. There are other agencies and persons who have much to contribute, but all can work better if there is some central focus of organization and planning. Institutions of higher education could provide that focus. Are they capable of moving beyond traditional routine preoccupations to enter with vigor into an education of learner-directed growth toward freedom? The demands of the disadvantaged, the immobility of the advantaged, the fears found in all, constantly threaten disaster. A vigorous use of American educational facilities could replace a pessimism for the foreboding future with a realistic hope for man's self-acquired ability to cope with the problems he has created.

Chapter II

WILL THE COLLEGE ACCEPT THE RESPONSIBILITY?

Few colleges are ready to undertake citizen education toward freedom. Most are sincere upholders of democracy. Their professors largely believe that their traditional activities are basic to liberty. But they are not yet ready to go into a full-scale program of fundamental education. Why? Because of self-imposed timidity. Their imaginations are limited by a loyalty to the familiar. Many are not aware of opportunities that lie beyond campus. Or, if they are, they assign responsibility to educators other than themselves.

In using the word "college," we are referring to the historic central task of higher education—general or liberal arts instruction for well-rounded free men. This basic purpose inspired the founding of the great universities, with their present masses of students, with their proliferation of professional schools and specialized research agencies. Every university possesses a general college as central core. The smaller, independent institutions boast of carrying this function even better, as one justification for their continued existence. "The college" is a common denominator of all higher education.

From the beginning, the college has dealt with those learnings that should fit students to become free men and women. It has pursued the liberalizing deal.

Expanding the Ideal

Colleges represent a culmination of the whole magnificent school system of America, the climax of the organized scheme of disciplined instruction for the young.

Schooling and/or Development

The characteristic concept of education held by those who deal with the young is schooling. The characteristic concept held by those who deal with adults should be development. Fundamental educators belong in the second category because they are concerned with all people, a majority of whom are adults. Schooling for the young is part of the problem of development. It should not determine the methods and activities which apply to adults. Education as development is the broader point of view, because it includes the concept of schooling. When college professors can lift their eyes to the broader understanding they can break out of the bonds imposed by their self-chosen limitations.

As long as education is thought of as something that occurs only within a school, the tendency is to limit the benefit to a chosen few, an elite. This contrasts with the developmental concept which makes the benefit available to everyone. Colleges characteristically deal with the surviving minority of many years of academic elimination.

As long as education is defined as schooling it is limited to a selected place for learning. For colleges this is a campus, contrasted with any place where people live out their lives. The privileged elite come to a protected atmosphere to develop in relative isolation from the kind of life they will live later. Benefit to learners tends to remain on campus.

As long as education is no more than schooling, it is limited to young years given over to formal learning. The standard for colleges is four years, ending in a "commencement," when post-educational life supposedly begins. This is contrasted with education as life-long development that ceases only when the learner ceases.

College people cling to the concept of education as schooling. They give a little thought to continued development of their graduates in alumni associations. They tend to ignore the vast majority of humanity except as these less-educated folk may become the followers of the few leaders they train. They fail to recognize that the overwhelming majority of humanity, denied the benefit of a college liberalizing education, will be less and less content to accept the leadership of a gently-bred elite. Even more than the academically privileged, those denied schooling need an education that frees. In

the modern world the liberalizing ideal should not remain an exclusive possession of the privileged.

The two concepts of education, schooling and development, are
equally legitimate. Both can be accepted by colleges. The first point
of view stresses subject-matter content as though skills and information were the essence of liberty. Its defenders give inadequate consideration to the individuals who must free themselves. The second
point of view stresses process of growth, as though specific skills and
information were unimportant. Its defenders give inadequate consideration to the subject-matter which people must learn in order to
continue the process of growth toward freedom. The excesses of each
point of view tend to be balanced by the other when both are accepted within the same institution.

A college can accept both concepts by carrying on programs for
two groups of learners. Education as schooling can continue for
students while education as development is organized for citizens.
Fundamental education can then become a legitimate purpose of the
college. The accumulated wisdom of the campus is made available
in a form that will stimulate all men toward self-development. The
traditional purposes of higher education can be better served when
students come into contact with citizens in normal locale of living.
Neither concept need displace the other. Each can serve the other as
the college comes to serve more adequately the needs of a turbulent
age.

Regaining Religious Emphasis

Development assumes direction. Men develop toward some ideal,
some scheme of values.

The liberal college lost a traditional direction-inspiring asset when
it abandoned religion as a central responsibility. Scholarship was
divorced from motivations to do the right or to serve the common
good. The loss of a religious focus helped to break the curriculum
into fragments, gave free rein to each subject-matter specialty to
pursue its own goals out of relationship to any concept of wholeness.

The acceptance of development as an aim of higher education calls
for some reintroduction of a religious emphasis. The impulse to be
cultivated is more universal than belief associated with a particular
creed or church or denomination. It is a faith, one that can govern
and judge life by intangible values. It has a gentler mood than the

stern New England conscience or the determination to evangelize the world to "our" image. It insists that there are basic decencies in all men, underdeveloped potentialities for good.

Religion is a scheme of values that pervades and gives meaning to all of life. As any college looks forward to humanity-wide educational responsibilities it will need to regain a religious emphasis; to provide vigorous and practical opportunity for students to create their own ethical focus; to evolve religious commitment that respects the citizens' search for the better.

The colleges abandoned a narrow religious emphasis little related to the problems of living. As educators for development they will search for a broad religious emphasis vigorous enough to give guidance to men and women who work in freedom for universal decencies.

THE NEGLECTED OPPORTUNITY

The neglected opportunity for the college lies in a courageous acceptance of responsibility for fundamental education. In so doing, it can recapture many of its historic purposes. It can re-relate these objectives and the subject-matter study that pursues them, to the world with which the students must contend. The neglected opportunity lies all about the college in accumulations of humanity, nearby and far away. A vigorous acceptance of the challenge of human development will allow each college to find a unique socially-significant focus for itself to help guide an era of change while serving the growth needs of learners.

Uniting the Quests

Freedom is the avowed purpose of both academic and fundamental education. Each effort is devoted to a quest for responsible maturity in people. Then why not unite them in a single program? A few institutions have begun combining the quests. Enough experience has accumulated to allay any fears that disciplinary academic instruction will be jeopardized when time is devoted to citizen development. The objectives are similar. The constituencies of learners and the educational methods differ. The opportunity to serve citizens need not be neglected because of apprehension that the proper education of students will be neglected.

Even though a college accepts fundamental education, it does not make radical changes in methods of on-campus instruction. Students and faculty work to expedite a process of education as development among citizens. But they do so under the requirements of education as schooling.

Discipline for students is still essential. They must fit into a curriculum, many elements of which are compulsory. The teacher remains a determiner of instructional material and method, and grants marks or grades or uses other means of approving excellence. The student advances up prescribed avenues of progress toward certain degrees or certifications. For the most part, the process remains teacher-dominated.

At certain points there is an encouragement of student choice and initiative. Such encouragement will be found in many other phases of good contemporary higher education. Students need to enter into many fundamental education activities as volunteers because they are poor helpers of others when under compulsion. There is also wide room for discussional difference of opinion when dealing with next steps in practical situations. Not even the professor knows the correct answer to many non-academic problems.

Students are still taught culture and abstract wisdom but as many as possible are given opportunity to test theory in the practice of real life. Some aspects of schooling are made more alive by application to people and their problems. There will always be more bookish learning taught than can ever emerge in practice, and this is good. Students are offered a few points of real experience for critical evaluation of some elements of intellectual learning. Their whole reaction to learning of abstractions may be made more intelligently critical by reference to a few experiences of real life that are related to academics.

Students are offered an opportunity to integrate their learnings and to find values-in-action within the simplest social unit that is basic to democracy, a community.

Most colleges will continue to give major effort to educating an elite to become leaders for democracy. But these few will more often be educated to work with rather than away from the majority of people. Students tend to gain respect for the inherent yet underdeveloped capacities of many kinds of people. They are encouraged to move away from cynical condemnation of the average, away from the expectation of dominating less-educated people for their own advantage. The leadership trained by colleges stands a better chance of being put to work in the service of democracy. Students and professors have opportunity to discover how many of their treasures of learning can be shared with those who have been denied such advantages.

Colleges may find a focal point for needed faculty and departmental cooperation. The focal point does not threaten the separate intellectual disciplines; it readapts them to serve the most important educational task which faces modern man.

Students indulging in fundamental education start with a class on the campus. They study about human beings, how they behave in groups, and how they develop. They discuss, in advance, the situation and the problems that they will encounter in trips off-campus. They go out to meet people, in individual conversations, in meetings, in periods of work together. In making contacts with citizens, their main purpose is not to instruct or to study people or to write reports and essays, although all of these activities may appear as by-products. Their main purpose is to be helpful. They expedite self-development by offering to push forward any legitimate community activity. Physical labor is the most obvious encouragement they can offer, but other more subtle and important helps should be kept in mind. Among these are the encouragement offered by believing in people, the attendance at meetings and joining in discussion with questions and ideas, and the bringing (upon request) of pertinent information from their more formal studies.

At a moment of success in a community project, the chairman of the activity expressed his gratitude to a professor in charge of students. "We are so grateful to you people for coming here to help us on this," said he. The community was raising money for a new public school building which was to be erected partly by labor contributed from the town and the college.

The professor replied, "Oh, we do not deserve the credit. You people here are doing the job."

"Yes, I know we are. But we never would have done anything if you and your students had not come down here to get us started. We have been talking about this sort of thing for years. We just needed the extra push you gave us to get going."

The citizen perceives college participation as a help to himself. The student frequently perceives his activity as an adventure, with social significance. The professor can perceive it all as an opportunity for speeding young learners toward a liberalizing maturity. In one community contact, students were laboring with local people to construct a road into an isolated section. A Catholic priest supporter of the enterprise said in a moment of grateful enthusiasm:

"This work that the students are doing is pure altrusim."

The professor in charge made reply, "No, it's not pure altruism."

"Well, why isn't it? These young people came a long way to help us, and are sweating out in the hot sun for the benefit of others."

"Yes, but they are getting something out of it. They are having a good time even though they are working hard. They are learning about life in a new environment. They are learning about people, how they act and grow."

"As I was saying, this is pure altruism," replied the priest.

Later the professor passed the comment on to the students. Their responses varied from incredulity to amusement. None would admit to any unusual virtue. One expressed the general conclusion of the rest. "We like it better when there is a lot of work to do."

Many kinds of activity invite student participation. A planning commission asks for help in making a real property inventory of the entire city as preliminary to formulation of a new master plan. A chamber of commerce requests help in making a survey of the history and present status of industry, labor supply, transportation and the like. A church council seeks a citywide survey of church membership. Government and private social welfare agencies ask for help in reducing juvenile delinquency, by collecting facts, by conducting clubs and recreation centers. A county reforestation project is started to conserve soil, water, and wild-life. Students join in a community chorus that builds local sense of togetherness. Citizens and students work together to improve relations between conflicting factions or races, or to conduct a forum for public discussion of controversial issues.

Whenever their newly-acquired academic skills prove useful to citizens (and only then) students focus formal learning upon the problem at hand. Historical, botanical, geologic, and economic facts are useful in application when needed. Mathematical, musical, and psychological skills are welcome when needed.

The city planning commission asked for and received gratefully a series of maps of the expansion of the city over many years, prepared by history students. Churches used data collected by sociology students and organized by mathematics classes. Farmers and public-spirited citizens enjoyed working with science students who helped them plant trees and construct conservation ponds. The possibilities of application of college teaching are limited only by the ingenuity of professors.

To persuade impatient students and instructors to withhold their wisdom until it will prove helpful is difficult. But the learning of such self-restraint is part of a liberalizing education for both. For a systematic outline of his subject-matter, the professor still depends on his text book or syllabus. For the application of his wisdom to real life, he depends upon the opportunities that community contact make available.

The whole student learning process is completed in classroom discussion. There the previous discussion, readings, related academic learning, experiences with citizens, and contributions of students are put together and interpreted. Each student is afforded an opportunity to arrive at an integration and understanding of his own, in the light of his emerging scheme of values. No learner is obligated to accept any interpretation offered by instructor or fellow student. He is obligated to attempt to arrive at an interpretation that makes sense to him, but is subject to the crossfire of criticism from fellow participants in the class discussion.

Such discussional freedom to differ is not unique to classes that grow from contact with developing citizens. But such classes are unique in that they can be conducted no other way. Whatever the assigned reports or readings, the variety of life found in real contacts imposes a necessity for difference of opinion on practical next steps and on long-run objectives to be sought.

Students contributing to fundamental education must be more than observers or continuers of present community functions. They become contributors to development. They encourage citizens to undertake activities, by their offers of help, by their evident belief in citizen ability. They, together with instructors, may suggest organization of new community committees when necessary or the taking on of new functions by those already in existence, or the broadening of purposes, or the growing on to higher ethical levels and more complicated responsibilities. The suggestions for change are offered by the raising of questions and the sketching in of alternative possibilities in meetings. In most of these guidance activities for citizens, the main initiative and skill are found in the professor rather than in the student. But the usefulness and gently persuasive quality of young people should never be underrated. The fact that they are obvious learners who are present to be helpful and to learn, makes their suggestions acceptable, because their recommendations can be rejected without embarrassment. If participation in fundamental education contributes to undergraduate growth, it aids citizens also, when instructors and students work in thoughtful harmony together.

The Tragedy of the Timid Approach

To some educators it may seem that a uniting of the quests for freedom may be achieved through the sending of classes off-campus in traditional field work. A much more elaborate responsibility is involved, if citizens are to be urged toward fundamental development and if students are to benefit by contact with important growth. The neglected opportunity will remain neglected unless there is commitment on the part of college administration and some members of a faculty to adventure boldly with an opportunity.

Growth toward freedom continues far beyond the normal span of semester-long or year-long classes or the normal four years of undergraduate work. If students are to benefit by contact with such growth, an agreement to continue cooperating with a particular program of community development over a span of years is necessary. Students, geared to shorter-time learning schedules, must come into a development project at different stages of progress. For the benefit of their understanding an account of previous steps taken and a projection into the future becomes necessary. A long-time commitment, possibly one of five to ten years, is thus involved for any college that gives serious consideration to the challenge.

Harassed by insufficient funds, a shortage of trained personnel, and increasing crowds of students that must be given the bare minimum of required courses, the colleges have a tendency to accept new obligations with an excess of caution. With full sympathy for administrators, there should be insistence that the development of underdeveloped peoples in the twentieth century is too important a matter to be hampered by timidity.

Field work in sociology is not enough. The expansion of work in anthropology or social psychology or adult education alone will not meet the need. A coordinating committee of already busy teachers or department heads cannot do an adequate job alone. Some courageous program closer to the central historic purpose of higher education is required.

PROGRAMS IN ACTION

A Bureau of Fundamental Education

The first recommended step for such a program is the setting up of an interdepartmental bureau or program assigned the task of developing activities and enthusiasm for fundamental education. This bureau may be brought into being by a committee of interested professors or department heads. It may be set up by the president and deans. Neither a committee nor the regular administrative staff alone can carry the responsibility, however. A separate integrative entity is needed, one which has the support of influential personalities and departments. The bold selection of a bureau and of adequate personnel to man it is a notification that the college is determined to go into the activity with vigor, that it does not propose to eliminate the activity when the inevitable criticisms and budget pressures arise.

A bureau of fundamental education should not be organized as a side-issue to an academic department. If attached to a social science division or to one school of a university, it should have freedom and authorization to roam over the entire institution, seeking cooperation from every academic subdivision. The functions of the bureau are two: to find or promote projects of self-improvement in communities and to entice faculty colleagues into participation in these activities with their students. In order to expedite these purposes, the bureau sets up a number of courses for study of and cooperation with human beings in native habitat. It promotes a variety of activities which frequently are not given academic credit, on-campus conferences that stimulate interest, and off-campus work periods that contribute to citizen growth. The bureau must be granted enough standing to command respect, and a sufficient budget to employ personnel and allow its activities to go forward.

The bureau becomes a promotional agency for fundamental education. We will refer to its personnel as "the promoter" or "the advocate," although "he" may be plural in many instances. He supports a new concept of education, quietly, gently, mainly on a basis of person-to-person understanding, and over a period of patient years. He often gives support in meetings by his silence and physical presence. Though he may become eloquent at times, he looks to colleagues to achieve new ideas of their own. We use the words "promoter" and "advocate" because the language does not provide a term for the persuader that seeks development toward self-chosen broader vistas.

Although full-time attention to the work of fundamental education is recommended, the promoter may indulge, from time to time, in teaching within his own specialty. Such a course of action grants him an acceptance of academic respectability among colleagues. His standing with them is important. If they reject him because he lacks advanced degrees or is too young or has no field of recognized competence or does not have an academic appointment that assures recognition, his persuasiveness is limited. He needs an appointment as a full professor; lower than a dean; something on a par with a department head but without the authority to command. He should be able to gain entrée to the attention of colleagues of every academic rank without power to demand acceptance of his ideas.

A promoter's function is not that of a salesman but of a stimulator. He provides ideas, experiences, and a vision, but he seldom expects his proposals to be adopted intact. He invites his colleagues to work toward an educational wholeness addressed to the needs of contemporary mankind. He is most successful not when his proposals are adopted by faculty vote, but when colleagues evolve ideas of their own that embody or are inspired by his vision.

A promoter is concerned about self-development of citizens; he is concerned also about self-development of faculty colleagues. If in impatience he demands compliance, he delays progress of his institution toward the goal he seeks. The analogy between community and campus is not complete, however. For professors, the latter is a place of employment, subject to the discipline of administration and trustees. The advocate of change must work within a hierarchical situation with established channels of communication and command. He exercises leadership, but he must be aware of and use the kind that will increase the self-choosing freedom of faculty colleagues.

A college cannot succeed with fundamental education unless its instructors are themselves growing toward greater responsible freedom. Yet few faculties will spontaneously adopt any such aims for their institution. The advocacy of a new idea must come from some stimulative source.

The advocate of fundamental education asks that the administration take one role of leadership, himself another. The first is top-level, policy-determining, authoritive, even when granting much right of decision to professors or students. The second is colleague-level, seeks to gain no more compliance than will be given voluntarily, seeks to stir initiative to accomplish new purposes. All he asks of administration is that it set up his bureau to function adequately, give fundamental education its blessing, then cast him loose to be persuasive. The administration dreams a dream, sets up an agency to make it real, clears the way, and then allows the promoter to win over colleagues to a broader interpretation of education.

As examples of top-level endorsement, consider two statements from institutional administrators. The first is from the president of a small college, the second from the chancellor of a university.

Through such an experience students gain a new appreciation of education. They see what it is for and what it can mean to them. Theoretical and applied learning meet. Emotion, thought, and action become fused, and the resulting enkindlement is something they can never forget.

By bringing together public and private educational enterprises, uniting the theoretical and vocational aspects of liberal education, and providing a laboratory for international, inter-racial, and intercultural exchanges, the Community Dynamics program implements the Earlham Idea. It expresses the Quaker philosophy of the College. It unites feeling, thought and action in a "wholistic" approach to learning. It provides also incentive in a self-help family-like atmosphere of college and community.

The Puerto Rican workcamp is already demonstrating the value of the liberal arts interne experience. There have been similar demonstrations— in nearby places in Indiana. Interdepartmental planning, fieldwork, seminars, course reports, suitable examinations, credit evaluation, tuition and laboratory fees all have bearing and should be given consideration by the Faculty and Board of Trustees. Theoretical and vocational education related to community needs and backed up by public institutions can bring new significance to liberal arts education in America.[1]

From the Chancellor of a cooperating university:

The University's participation in the camp led to the recommendation that a similar program be developed and eventually incorporated into our curriculum. [He then goes into detail about the setting up of the activity with budgetary allotment and appointment of a director.] . . . if this program is expanded there will be opportunity for more students to participate. This summer new camp sites will be explored with a view to future expansion.

[1] Thomas E. Jones, President of Earlham College, in a report to the Faculty and Trustees, dated July 1954.

The objective examinations and the personal interviews at the beginning and end of the camp sessions show the effect which this activity has produced in varying degrees on the students. Changes in the social attitudes of the students were observed, and in some cases, they reconsidered their programs, finding new fields of interest for their studies.

Although this activity is still in an experimental stage, the educational value which it has demonstrated up to the present, indicates that it should be continued.[2]

Part of the administrative blessing for fundamental education activity consists of setting up an adequate bureau. Part consists of continuing support over a period of years, for professors, like other men, change their values and activities slowly. Another part consists of developing creative faculty meetings in which the promoter can present his case from time to time, can be part of a stream of discussion that interprets faculty experience and examines a curriculum that can be modified and remodified to meet changing times.

Service Areas

The personnel of the bureau, in consultation with administrators and cooperating colleagues, chooses geographic areas for fundamental education attention. In such territories smaller localities can be pinpointed and progress can be encouraged and studied over a period of years. The primary service area, in most instances, is one within a convenient radius of the campus as center.

Size of the primary area is difficult to prescribe. Here is a college in a sparsely settled section of the mountain states. The radius of its chosen service area is 250 to 300 miles; students and professors go out on assignment for several days. Here is a metropolitan college in a large city. The radius of its area is approximately 20 city blocks. The writers' personal experience, so far, limits them in general to a radius of 50 miles, with a notable exception, far away. The limit of domestic contacts is determined by motor trips of one day's duration.

Variety should be an important factor in choosing a secondary area. A city college might deliberately seek an additional rural situation even though far away, and the opposite might be true of the rural institution. Interest in special problems might supersede convenience in travel, such as a chance to cooperate with good government in

---

[2] Jaime Benitez, Chancellor of the University of Puerto Rico from his annual report to the Superior Education Council. May 1955, p. 97.

operation, a chance to work with some handicapped people, an opportunity for students to become familiar with several different cultural backgrounds. The problem of maintaining good public relations with certain supporters of the college is also worthy of consideration.

Rural Areas

Because of location or connections, many colleges will want to operate in rural areas. All that wish to serve humanity should be, for the majority of men (outside the United States) still live in villages, depending upon agriculture for a living.

Rural life in an industrial nation like the United States comes to resemble urban life more and more as time goes on. As a nation and its food-production industrialize, the experience of rural community life which once came automatically, is lost. This story has been told elsewhere.[3] There are exceptions to this trend, those underprivileged sections where an unmechanized agriculture is still the most important contributor to livelihood.

Colleges that seek rural communities will rapidly be forced to conclude that the idyllic setting of nostalgic memory is largely literary. Other related problems appear—a population less tied to a particular location, more likely to commute daily to a job or to move the whole family to new employment opportunities. Characteristic city problems may appear. Much of the countryside is becoming rurban (rural plus urban). Such changes are truly rural; they affect the lives of real human beings in an age of uncertainty.

In addition some experience with clearly underdeveloped rural folk in the United States is recommended for those colleges that plan to work within foreign service areas. There are domestic areas in the mountains, among sharecroppers, and elsewhere in which the human need is similar to that found in underdeveloped nations abroad.

Urban Areas

Urban areas are important to fundamental educators because they are pace-setters of change, both good and bad. The contrasts with village life are not differences of kind but rather of size and complexity. If the educator is to deal with the problems of real people

[3] William W. Biddle, *The Cultivation of Community Leaders* (New York: Harper & Brothers, 1953), Chap. III.

in modern times, he will consider rural and urban situations as inter-related.

The college will discover certain problems more evident in city environments than in rural areas. There is usually less concern for the welfare and growth of the individual; the citizen tends to be lost in a vast anonymity of the hive. Life is complicated by a greater tendency toward organized crime, gambling, and vice, and the corruption of politics that arises from such enterprises. The universal problems of child care, delinquency, housing, church life, and education are made more complicated by larger populations and the difficulty of obtaining a workable community autonomy within the control of local citizens.

The fundamental educator in the city will have to accept the disturbing necessity for working with several different social units covering the same people. Every city dweller lives within several potential communities, each of which is a focus of interest that may challenge his participation at some time. Thus, if citizens are concerned with a problem of their children's education, the unit of action may be the elementary or high school district. If it is a matter of politics, the unit may be the voting precinct; if a matter of housing, it may be the city block. There is no single community commanding loyalty as was true in the rural life of the past. (This multiplicity of foci for loyalty is beginning to appear in rural life as city influences have their effect in the country.) Nevertheless, the educator seeks to encourage the development of social units which will allow co-operative control. He does this by promoting collective action looking toward general improvement. But he and his students must not be alarmed if the geographic distribution of men's loyalties shift with the problem toward which the action is directed.

Work in an urban service area brings many of the most pressing problems of modern men sharply to the attention of students and professors. They must be careful, however, not to study these difficulties as "social pathologies" which can be cared for by the properly designated social welfare agencies. This professional worker's approach tends to reduce the already diminished citizen to an even smaller stature.

The anonymity, the obscuring of the individual, the lack of any single focus of community loyalty, these are increasingly the plight of modern man everywhere. If college learners can wrestle with the complexities of city life, if they can help to reawaken an active sense of community in the confusion of a rootless population, they can begin to set the pattern for an increase in freedom for all men.

Foreign Areas

Most colleges are interested in international affairs, but mainly at the top diplomatic level. That their students and staff could influence lives of ordinary citizens at the level of their daily lives has not occurred to most higher educators.

Every college should include at least one outreach of contact within a culture foreign to its own. Whether the college be predominantly rural or urban in domestic emphasis, it needs the perspective which can be gained only by experience with people of another culture. In general, those already working in this field will welcome a newcomer institution which proposes to assume a fundamentally educational responsibility.

In dealing with people of a strange environment, the college and its staff have an opportunity to match their educational wits against the serious problems that beset the human race. By developing a methodology to cope with illiteracy, superstition, and prejudice in a strange setting, they develop new perspective about domestic situations. The flexibility needed by the educator is developed by variety of experiences when attitudes of tolerance, appreciation of the other person, and gradualness in approach can be transferred from one social situation to another.

Suppose the following circumstances became reality within the near future: That each of the hundreds of colleges and universities in the United States developed at least one community laboratory of fundamental education in some land beyond the borders of the nation; that each situation in another culture was an independent enterprise of the responsible institution and therefore free from pressure toward uniformity and political propaganda; that the support of such enterprises was regarded as an integral part of each institution's budget; that the American college worked in harmony with educational forces in the host country. The impact upon education in this nation would be incalculable, but would be minor as compared with the positive effect upon international relations. Higher education would begin to make a person-to-person contribution to the achievement of world peace, without which the best efforts of states-men at the diplomatic level may prove unavailing.

If college fundamental educators are to serve mankind's need for growth, they will not be content to serve conveniently located, nearby aggregations of humanity alone. If they hope to bring a well-rounded education to students, they will give thought to service in several contrasting areas. They will limit efforts to specific projects but will spread the variety.

Experimentation with Methods

There are as yet no generally approved methods for combining student and citizen education.[4] This fact gives the promoter an oppor-tunity to enlist the best thinking of his colleagues to experiment. Some will be frightened at the lack of assured precedent. A small minority will be intrigued by the freedom which newness grants them. In either case, the need for experimental flexibility should be welcomed and regarded as permanent. Each accumulation of humanity, even in a single service area, presents a different problem. Each educational institution should seek its own unique contribution, though much mutual help is available in exchange of ideas from one college to another.

At the point of flexibility in method the promoter needs to develop some self-discipline. Out of his own fear of the unknown or lack of trust in colleagues he may seek to gain blanket endorsement for his ideas. He may conclude that he is in the position of the sower in the Biblical parable. He hopefully scatters his seeds of (to him) obvious truth only to have them fall upon the stony ground of faculty in-difference or to have them overcome by the weeds and tares of tradi-tional preoccupation and academic "busywork." He may be inclined to forget that even good soil varies in composition from one location to another and that no two academic fields will ever produce the same crop. But then his colleagues are not soil. They are intelligent human beings who deserve the respect he will show them by enlisting their enthusiasm to work out a unique balance of methods for each community situation and for each college.

A characteristic balance of opportunities and limitations is often found in a small, independent college. There size and a more direct personal relationship with colleagues, administrators, and trustees

[4] For detailed discussion of some methods now in use, see Chaps. V and VI.

make for flexibility. On the other hand, a diminutive budget and the desperate struggle for sufficient funds to keep the institution going tend to make any new activity unwelcome. The promoter will find great opportunity to cross traditional lines of academic demarcation, his friendships and personal contacts extending to every discipline and to top-level offices. Such freedom to range widely (even within a limited space) makes integration of higher education easier. There is an understanding, based upon an active camaraderie, of other people with markedly different interests. Faculty meetings can come to resemble direct democracy of the town-meeting variety if those who conduct and contribute to them have sufficient imagination and skill.

Usually, however, the promoter will find it necessary to accept a smaller salary than would be possible in a larger institution. He may have fewer facilities to use (no college-owned transportation, little equipment, limited publication opportunities, and so on). He may have less personal recognition than association with a big-name university would automatically grant. But if his work is good enough and his understanding of fundamental education humanitywide, he may find that the prestige of his contribution is not limited by the size of the institution which provides a base of operation.

As a colleague-level leader within the smaller institution, the promoter will face his own peculiar array of difficulties. He will try to move institutional thinking from constant worry over budgets, from adherence to traditionally-defined learning, to a vision of challenging new opportunities for service. He will strive to make clear that his program represents not a threat of rivalry, but a new chance for every educational function to contribute to a renewed contemporary usefulness. He will hope to discover in time, that the reorientation of his college has attracted new financial support. He will realize that the fact of smallness and greater flexibility gives his institution a freer scope to lead with new developments in higher education.

Within a university the promoter faces a different balance of opportunity and hindrance. The variety is great, from privately endowed institutions that frequently stress "pure" learning, to those that are publicly-supported and must perforce stress more practical applications of wisdom. In general, with a larger budget there is more leeway for adjustment and reallocation of funds. On the other hand, there is greater institutional inflexibility; separate schools and divisions have fixed obligations which must be met each year; it is often easier to continue a traditional job or activity (even if its usefulness has diminished) than to introduce a new function. The massive momentum of ongoing programs is not easy to deflect. Each established program within the greater enterprise tends to have a permanent and separate existence of its own, irrespective of the purpose of the whole.

The democracy of a university tends to be of the representative type. Coordination occurs through a meeting together, usually of department heads, deans, and other top administrators. Faculty meetings of the whole seldom take place; instead there are meetings of separated schools, each devoted to its own profession, or teaching and research interest, or subdivision of learning. Movement toward integration of education comes as a result of committee meetings among hierarchically-chosen representatives. The promoter of fundamental education is likely to find himself a servant of a committee of administrators and academic elders. His autonomy is therefore limited; his freedom to approach his colleagues is curtailed; he has fewer opportunities to stimulate the rank-and-file teacher who must become an active participant in the work. More than in a small institution, he needs a position of recognized standing in order to meet members of a high-level coordinating committee as an equal.

Financial compensation is more likely to be adequate in a university, as is the personal prestige that comes from association with a big name. There is likely to be more equipment available as well as a larger array of personnel from which to choose cooperators. But expenditures for new activities are more hemmed about by paper restrictions, requisitions, higher echelon approvals, and legal vetoes; colleagues are inspired with new ideas more slowly because they are seldom met face-to-face. The possibilities for new development are greater because there is more to work with. But the more elaborate array of facilities and personnel brings about a greater internal divisiveness and a more pronounced institutional inflexibility.

In such a situation, the advocate of fundamental education may ask that the activity be set up as another graduate-level specialty. The program should have a high enough recognition to allow it to be utilized by medical school and agricultural college, by general education and by graduate school. Otherwise it cannot serve as a stimulant for integration. The promoter attempts to move the institution from mere continuance of entrenched schools and divisions toward a gradual coordination that will involve as many separately-existing activities as possible and as many individual instructors as can be encouraged to volunteer. The adoption of new policy occurs at the administrative committee level. The personal involvement of working instructors follows more slowly.

Despite the tendency to bog down with its own complication and institutional machinery, a university has a unique opportunity in fundamental education. It is usually to the university with big operations and a big reputation that governments, industries, farmers, churches, and communities turn for help. Many applications of theoretical knowledge are already being carried forward before the promoter appears upon the scene. These await his insight to become more closely integrated around basic human need.

The realization of unique possibilities for any institution rests upon developing a faculty that will rise, of its own volition, to the challenge of developing humanity. How does such a faculty develop? The chief responsibility rests upon the promoter of fundamental education.

Winning Over a Faculty

Any advocate faces a paradox. He asks that his function be set up with sufficient standing to command the respect of colleagues, yet he wishes to avoid having his program regarded as a rival academic fragment, another department of a college or school of a university. His colleagues tend to classify his efforts into such traditional categories. He may find himself vacillating between his desire for recognized status and his desire for coordination of all learning to serve human need. Though the dilemma may never be entirely overcome, it can be reduced by personal friendship with many faculty members.

The loyalty that each professor feels toward his own specialty of learning is not peculiar to professors. It is related to the insecurity of modern life that leads men to cling to the job or narrow field in which each feels competent. Professors may find it hard to believe that any situation of development which is controlled by learners (that is, citizens) can be truly educational.

Integration of diverse interests and diverse learnings does not come just from talking together. It comes from new experience digested in talking; from working together on common projects that each person and each specialty can serve. The key to winning over a faculty is to be found in active participation in community projects. This experience is carried back to faculty gatherings for criticism, comment, and reorganization of thinking. Gradually, out of such experience, the insecurity that calls for separateness is replaced with a new security—in people, in their ability to grow in competence.

The severest critics will frequently accept an invitation to participate when an invitation is extended. If they participate they become supporters even when their own academic fields are not called upon.

A chemistry professor became a supporter because a student convinced him that a type of community participation represented the best of religion in action. The head of a university research bureau became enthusiastic because "young people need an experience of practical democracy that is governed by ideals." An English teacher wanted to take part in community workcamp activities in distant places because an opportunity to do so had come to his friend who taught Spanish. Another English instructor came closer to his own field of competence when he gave endorsement to community contacts for students because, as a result, they "now have something to write about" in papers.

When the students' usefulness in the community comes closer to a recognized academic skill, the professor usually discovers a broadening of his own point of view. A history instructor was willing to assign some of his students to write an account of certain historical backgrounds of a developing community. This research job was supported by local citizens because they felt the process of collecting information would be interesting and the resulting report would support their purposes. But the professor was made uncomfortable by the research methods necessarily employed. He, a top-grade research scholar, was accustomed to working in the quiet of a university library. He had never collected historic data in musty old attics or courthouses or, with even less accuracy, from the uncertain memories of old people. For a time he could not persuade himself that such research had merit. Eventually he learned to interpret accounts from such sources. He broadened his concept of historical research to apply to real life.

The instances of broadened professional perspectives can be multiplied and found in almost every academic department. The mathematician who found that his skill was helpful in compiling community self-surveys could be mentioned, as could the musician who came to appreciate his field as a contributor to local loyalty in a volunteer chorus, or the political science instructor who discovered that some of the high-level processes of national conflict could be observed and described in simpler form in villages near the home campus. In no instance did the professor find his entire field represented in community activity. But that field could be made more vital by discovering some local adaptation to the needs of citizens.

A biology professor presents an outstanding example of progress toward enthusiastic support for fundamental education. When a rural community project had need for erection of many sanitary privies, he was asked to supply working plans for such essential farm out-buildings. His first reaction was one of chagrin. Though he admitted that such information logically should come from his department, his textbooks did not cover the subject. He confessed to a feeling of unease at his ignorance. He went to work to rectify the gap in his knowledge, writing to health authorities and government agencies. Eventually he collected a commendable file of information about sanitation in less-developed rural areas. Three years later he became an active participant in a community project that installed some hundreds of sanitary privies. The people profited by his knowledge and eagerness to promote better health. He and his students became known on campus, at this time, as "privy councillors." They installed the first two such sanitary facilities in an underprivileged section and had the pleasure of seeing the idea accepted by virtually an entire population. Needless to say, he developed an abiding enthusiasm for community fundamental education.

It is good for college instructors to sit quietly in community meetings and listen to citizens wrestle with their problems, to wonder how they can contribute to an on-going process they do not control, to discover that their answers to problems are inapplicable or rejected by the meeting.

Said a student to a professor after a community meeting, "Weren't you worried about their opinion of you? Didn't you want them to realize that your point of view was the correct one?" Said the professor, "You know, that is interesting. I was wondering so much what I could say to help those people that I forgot about posing as the expert. *I said the thing that I thought would help them move toward a solution of their problem."*

The Fate of the Advocate

A footnote about the promoter is in order. His function is important in the adoption of fundamental education by any college.

But he must avoid delusions of grandeur. His colleagues will usually help in this matter. He will not become the winner of any popularity contest, because he will be looked upon as a bit odd. Since his classification will be difficult to describe until coordinators become more common on campuses, colleagues must worry about him, apologize for him, defend or attack him. They may look upon him as a gadfly, although a gentle one. They will seldom choose him as chairman of or place him upon the more important committees. Nevertheless, his influence may prove to be strong in time.

Any successful promoter must be prepared to offer ideas to colleagues with expectation that many of them will be rejected. His security must not rest upon personal prominence. He may expect to have some of those ideas reappear in the proposals of others with no credit to himself. The credit is unimportant as long as people develop. Like any good teacher, he works through others, individuals, committees, a special group set up to plan for development activities, faculty meetings. His triumph is theirs.

If the promoter is patiently persistent and keeps his sense of humor and accepts his rebuffs with plans for the next steps to be taken, he will succeed in bringing about favorable changes. He will find that his colleagues come to tolerate and like him as a person even if they examine his proposals with skepticism. They will come to respect the new vistas he opens up to their thinking even while they protest that the view is uncomfortable—but exciting. In time their imaginations will begin to soar toward the great educational challenge of the age. And a faculty then will begin to formulate its own unique contribution to the difficult task of promoting human self-development.

An End of Academic Isolation

Colleges need not continue their isolation from the world. A few, and a few more, stir with discomfort, reach out for more responsible goals. Some are beginning to understand that if ethically-guided intelligence can solve men's problems, higher education must accept responsibility for fundamental education.

The liberal tradition will be enhanced by invitation to student participation with citizens. Students will be urged to seek an education that honors self-chosen values.

By uniting fundamental and liberal education, colleges will bring more vitality to learning for students while aiding citizen search for freedom. The proposed new responsibility does not represent an added burden so much as a revision of present practice. Colleges can again become places of lively challenge to young people, but only as they pit their wisdom and skill against the worries and frustrations of an age in turmoil.

If freedom is to survive and spread it must do so in the hands of more people than existing colleges can educate on campus. Colleges will be able to serve the ideals that founded them by bursting beyond the walls that contain them. The time has come for higher education to make the development that frees, available to all who will accept it.

Chapter III

A COMMUNITY FOR GROWTH

When a college seeks to be useful beyond the campus, it properly turns to community experts for guidance. What does it find? Confusion. The experts cannot agree upon a definition of community nor upon the proper assemblage of people which might be utilized.[1]

There is no generally-accepted definition of community in modern times because there is little satisfying experience of community. The historical concepts are useful, as history. But people all over the world are moving away from the villages and small towns of an agrarian civilization toward an industrial-urban way of life, possibly toward other goals too dimly in the future to describe. Neither the departing communities of memory nor contemporary conglomerations of humanity as they are will serve as satisfactory places of operation for fundamental educators.

It is necessary, however, to examine the variety of concepts found in the thinking of those who work with communities. Are there common elements? What elements of definition and what realities of local life open the way for educational growth toward freedom? The confusion is reduced when the opinions of the experts are arranged in an ordered array of types.

AN EXPERT'S TYPOLOGY

Each expert tends to use the word "community" to refer to a different characteristic accumulation of people, depending upon the local situation which he admires or with which he has had most experience. The belligerence between experts is reduced when each

[1] See George A. Hillery, Jr., "Definitions of Community," *Rural Sociology*, June 1955, p. 111 ff.

point of view can be accepted as legitimate though not exclusively correct.

Decentralists

When some writers refer to community they have in mind an ideal group of people deliberately brought together to create a more blessed relationship. Such assemblages are almost always small, at least in beginnings; they may consist of no more than half a dozen families. They are usually rural. They are offered as an escape from the ugliness and unpleasantness of city life. Many such historic enterprises have been organized around a particular religious cult, The Oneida Community in New York State, The New Harmony Community in Indiana, the Mormon settlements in Utah. The Koinonia Community in Georgia is a contemporary example. In more recent years the religious sectarian element has diminished, but the search for an ideal community of escape is still observable. The impulse has received new strength from the fear of atomic attack upon huge populations. To the yearning for an ideal life has been added the yearning for survival.

It is not possible to list upholders of this point of view (or of any of the others) with full assurance that those listed will be happy about the classification. Names are mentioned, therefore, with the assumption that those classified belong primarily in a particular category, in the judgment of the writers. The people and organizations are meant to be characteristic, not complete. Apologies are offered in advance for any injustices of commission or omission.

Among the upholders of the decentralist point of view are the Fellowship of Intentional Communities,[2] *The Interpreter*, a publication edited by Mildred J. Loomis, and Ralph Borsodi.[3] At times Baker Brownell [4] sounds as though he had some sympathy for this position though he belongs even more surely in the next category.

Rural and Small Town Practitioners

Some of the most outstanding successes in re-creation of community spirit are to be found in small town and rural life. The achieve-

---

[2] Community Service, Inc., Box 243, Yellow Springs, Ohio.

[3] See his book, *Flight from the City* (Suffern, N. Y.: School of Living Inc., 1947).

[4] In his book, *The Human Community* (New York: Harper & Brothers, 1951).

ment grows partly out of the fact that present-day rural centers, though changing, more closely resemble traditional ideas of local living than do larger population centers. There is a yearning for a lost (or failing) pattern of living that can be recaptured for a time and utilized. The self-contained village, the New England town, the pioneer center of local loyalty, these all were historically basic to American concepts of democracy. Some counterpart adaptation has important meaning for the continuance of democracy in modern times.

The contributors to this point of view are legion. Some are advocates. Others are adherents who have no aversion to carrying the same spirit into cities, if possible. The strong advocates have some affinities to the Decentralists. Some tend to hold that the rescue of human freedom rests upon a return to small center life, often with the implication that city-dwellers are well-nigh lost. In one form or another this note runs through Brownell, Arthur Morgan,[5] and H. Clay Tate.[6] It is to be found in the description of the Montana Study made by Richard Poston.[7] Griscom Morgan, The Community Service Inc., which he heads, and his publication, *Community Service News*, should be included.

The workers in smaller centers who do not exclude or who carry their point of view over to cities, include Poston in a later book,[8] the Ogdens,[9] Otto Hoiberg,[10] the Biddles,[11] and Irwin Sanders.[12] These writers try to find in the smaller situation a pilot laboratory for developing methods that can be adapted to other larger and more complicated situations.

Neighborhood Operators

When larger numbers of people are involved, the small town or

[5] *A Business of My Own* (Yellow Springs, Ohio: Community Services, Inc., 1946).

[6] *Building a Better Home Town* (New York: Harper & Brothers, 1954).

[7] *Small Town Renaissance* (New York: Harper & Brothers, 1950).

[8] *Democracy is You* (New York: Harper & Brothers, 1953).

[9] Jean and Jess Ogden, *Small Communities in Action* and *These Things We Tried* (New York: Harper & Brothers, 1946, 1947).

[10] *Exploring the Small Community* (Lincoln, Neb.: University of Nebraska Press, 1955).

[11] *The Cultivation of Community Leaders* (New York: Harper & Brothers, 1953).

[12] *Making Good Communities Better* (Lexington, Ky.: University of Kentucky Press, 1950).

even the small city is no longer a useful instrument. The neighborhood may become the unit of organization with which the developer works. The experience of living in a neighborhood is not one found in huge metropolitan centers only. It is found in rural areas also, in surburbs, and in the ill-defined area of "rurban" life. As the importance of small-town centers has diminished, as the individual has tended to become lost in the city, awareness of neighborhood loyalty has seemed to provide basis for a usable educational unit.

The Ohio Farm Bureau has experimented successfully with rural neighborhood organization. The College in the Country of West Georgia College has developed such neighborhoods under direction of R. Carson Pritchard. Some descriptions of both rural and city progress will be found in McKee's, The People Act.[13] The Biddles and the Ogdens have both worked in country and city neighborhoods. The Murrays [14] have developed neighborhood activities in large cities, as has The School of Education at New York University and The Community Service Division at the College of the City of New York. In Kansas City a neighborhood organization is based upon elementary school districts which pyramid up to high school districts and finally to a citywide citizen's council. Neighborhood houses or settlements have a long and honorable history. In Chicago neighborhood citizen units have been developed under encouragement of The University of Chicago.[15] Perhaps the most ambitious national program is that of ACTION (American Council to Improve Our Neighborhoods).[16] This organization devotes itself exclusively to city problems. It encourages neighborhood initiative over the entire nation.

All over the world problem situations of rootless people can be handled through utilization of neighborhood units. In a restless age the number of situations increase of human beings torn from traditional ties to place or to other persons, assembled together in unfriendly jumble without new ties to replace those lost. Problems of disease, delinquency, and lack of responsibility can be handled as these people develop a sense of community with each other and with

[13] Elmore McKee (New York: Harper & Brothers, 1955).

[14] Clyde E. Murray, Group Work in Community Life (New York: Association Press, 1954), and, with Janet P. Murray, Guide Lines for Group Leaders (New York: Whiteside, Inc., 1954).

[15] Herbert Thelen, Dynamics of Groups at Work (Chicago: Univ. of Chicago Press, 1954).

[16] Box 462, Radio City Station, New York 20, N. Y.

more permanent neighbors. The neighborhood as a unit can be used to serve those who have lost intimate experience of community ties as well as permanent inhabitants.

Special Interest Groups in City

Certain city problems are beyond the scope of neighborhood units to handle. Smaller numbers of citizens can be involved in pursuing study of these problems and in taking action to solve them. Interested citizens will seldom all be concentrated in any one section of the city. Though their places of residence may be widely scattered, they will want to come together around a common enthusiasm. Such foci of interest are music, foreign affairs, mental hygiene, better schools, a metropolitan church, a hobby activity, study or discussion of some special field. All such interests are legitimately referred to as community activities. They can be utilized by an educator as social units for stimulation of educational growth.

Among the special interests are those that cluster about social work. The Murrays represent this emphasis, as does Clarence King.[17] Another area is that of the schools. Harry E. Moore,[18] Seay and Crawford,[19] and Campbell and Ramseyer [20] have written upon community support for public schools and their utilization for citizen development. At the University of Indiana a program of adult community education goes forward that utilizes schools, hospitals, churches, and libraries, under direction of Paul Bergevin. Libraries and churches are active in their own right. Labor unions conduct classes and have an extensive literature. A host of special interest activities are carried forward by a great variety of adult education enterprises, classes, discussion groups, and committees to take action in solution of specific problems.

One type of citywide special interest group needs mention—the reform association. Though the promoters of a particular program of improvement would desire the participation of all citizens, their single-minded devotion to a "cause" often forces them to become a

[17] Your Committee in Community Action (New York: Harper & Brothers, 1952).

[18] Nine Help Themselves (Austin, Texas: University of Texas, 1955).

[19] Maurice F. Seay and Ferris H. Crawford, The Community School (Michigan: Superintendent of Public Instruction, 1954).

[20] Roald F. Campbell and John A. Ramseyer, The Dynamics of School-Community Relationships (New York: Allyn and Bacon, 1955).

pressure group. In spite of this difficulty, however, there is room for the special interest group that presses for reform when the methods used look toward participative community and individual growth. The interest may be special; it should not be selfish. There are two criteria that distinguish the selfish from the altruistic interest. First is the manner of organization. Is membership in the group open to all who care to join? Second is the matter of method. Does the concerned minority seek to win over voluntary participation rather than impose its predetermined solution upon a quiescent "public"?

Growth toward the wholeness of community experience can begin with minority pursuit of special altruistic interest. The problem is to extend interest and participation beyond the initial devoted minority, in widening circles.

Big City Advocates

If small town advocates become over-enthusiastic in their condemnation of metropolitan centers, big city advocates can become equally indifferent to the significance of the lesser places. Each can reach the point of assuming that the unit of population with which he works represents the norm of human existence. Much will be gained when each can reduce the extravagance of claims, can recognize the contribution of the other, and can agree to work in harmony with those who utilize other concepts of community.

The city as determiner of customs, fashion, and taste tends to be on the side of mass control. The encouragement of unique individual development is neglected. Nevertheless the great city is a unit of educational operation which cannot be ignored. The opportunity for the fundamental educator is twofold; to break the mass into sub-units that can give scope to individual development for those problems that can be handled on a neighborhood basis; to encourage increase of citizen participation in solution of those problems which must be handled on citywide scale.

To refer to a metropolis of hundreds of thousands or millions as a community does not satisfy many "pure" definers. Yet action together and common usage demand serious consideration for this large unit. Many such huge centers have an annual Community Chest Drive to raise funds for philanthropic purposes. The "Red Feather" agencies thus supported look to the alleviation and improvement of community problems. The city planners think in terms of over-all community need, looking beyond their maps of a city and its physical structures to neighborhoods and to the people who live in them. Since cities can afford to employ more specialized experts, planners, dispensers of relief, social workers, enforcers of law, they come to depend upon these paid functionaries. If citizens are to be educated by active participation in the affairs that affect their lives, they must be pulled into some phases of the activities handled by these employed and competent professionals.

Among those who are giving constructive thought to the growth of people in cities are the Murrays and Clarence King, and others connected with such universities as Chicago, Columbia, and New York. The American Society of Planning Officials has been moving in its thinking.[21] Arthur Hillman has attempted to tie together the concepts of planning and community development.[22] Community organization is a specialty of social work training of long-standing respectability. It is addressed for the most part to problems of cities where professional social workers are employed in considerable number. There are many textbooks in this field.[23]

There is no reason to believe that people in large numbers will move out of cities. Metropolitan centers will exist for a long time (unless wiped out by disaster). Educators interested in the development of people should go where people are to be found. The city is a community educational unit to be used. Its complications, sharp contrasts of wealth, and sheer weight of numbers challenge the best that educators have to offer.

Any Corporate Body

Those who would use communities for educative purposes cannot stop with metropolitan accumulations as the largest geographic units under consideration. Planners, and community educators have dealt with counties, regions, states and even nations. (Worldwide planning waits upon worldwide political harmony.) Though they may not refer to these larger units as communities, they and certain other community-centered people and agencies will offer their services to these larger bodies.

[21] ASPO, 1313 East Sixteenth St., Chicago 37, Ill.

[22] *Community Organization and Planning* (New York: Macmillan, 1950).

[23] A recent good one is Murray G. Ross, *Community Organization Theory and Principles* (New York: Harper & Brothers, 1955).

Educators should become aware of the planning movement which presses, by the logic of modern necessity, toward consideration of even larger areas. In an interdependent industrial age, some kind of city and regional and national planning is inevitable. The problem is not to oppose the trend blindly, but to guide it into democratic channels. Only by recapturing and strengthening local autonomies within a planning area, so that these contribute to the planning, can individual citizens come to contribute to their own future.

The concept of community being used here is ill-defined. It seems to be almost any corporate body that cares to make research studies (defined as fact-gathering), and to press toward improvement (loosely-defined). Two such agencies are Community Research Associates, Inc.[24] and The National Council for Community Improve-provement.[25] The facts gathered are useful; the impulse to improvement is to be commended. This concept does not make communities available as educative instruments, however, because the search for facts and for improvement tends to ignore people. The educator, aware of processes of human development, needs to come more actively into the picture.

Community in General

Concepts of community are incomplete unless place is left for a general or generic use of the word. In the thinking of many people, community refers to a vaguely-approved togetherness, sense of belonging to some important association, to being friends and having common purposes. Perhaps sociologists and anthropologists would prefer to abandon such nebulous usages. But many people, some well-educated, will apparently continue to refer to such things as community of interest among men of goodwill, or among those united by such a "cause" as anti-communism. Community then becomes almost synonymous with common purposes that could move toward brotherhood—sometimes a brotherhood held together only by a common enemy.

The generic use of the word does not necessarily allow community to evaporate into complete vagueness. When a university inaugurates a statewide or regionwide program of community development en-

[24] Bradley Buell, *Community Planning for Human Services* (New York: Columbia University Press, 1952).
[25] Paul Brown Bldg., 818 Olive Street, St. Louis 1, Mo.

couraging many other agencies and institutions of higher education to utilize local social units, it is using the word legitimately. It is avoiding a more exact definition lest too specific a concept hamper experimentation. It should be seeking for a generally-desirable type of relationship among men and within their associations. When diplomats seek to foster an Atlantic Community or a Western Hemisphere Community among nations, there is meaning and merit to the idea. The ultimate expansion of local experience of living and working together in self-chosen harmony is (until space travel discovers other civilized creatures in the universe) worldwide community.[26]

All the concepts listed are useful and to be honored. Faithfulness to any single concept, as though the others did not exist, implies an arrogant naïveté in the user. The whole field of community development would be benefited if the developers could accept the full gamut of uses. The discussion of their work would be clearer if they designated which social unit they were utilizing in any given discussion.

From Definition to Utility

When discussing community as locus for education, the different concepts must, however, be evaluated. Those which encourage greater attention to the developing individual are preferable. The difficulty is this: those who hope for a satisfactory definition seek to describe something that already exists. They desire to locate an existing community which they can use.

A college entering the field of fundamental education must find some (in time more than one) local accumulation of people with which to operate. It will seek a social unit that is convenient in size and location, one that is understandable as a result of study, one whose citizens might prove educable, one in which person-to-person interaction between citizens and with college people is possible. The definition in terms of size and boundaries will be made by the inhabitants, in their actions. None the less, the college will push for educational experience in divisions and subdivisions of humanity which are meaningful to learners. Attempt will be made to break great populations into smaller units. Then, for larger problems, these

[26] See, for example, Karl W. Deutsch, *Political Community at the International Level* (New York: Random House, 1955).

units will be reunited, with respect for individual initiative, into the larger organizations which interdependence demands.

The Educative Community

When attempting to develop communities as educative instruments, colleges again may ask advice from those experienced in such work—adult educators and community developers. Among these experienced professionals they will find a heavy reliance upon production of mass materials and packaged programs for instruction of adults. The assumption for many seems to be that, having selected a community in which to operate, the responsibility will be discharged by applying large amounts of preprepared instruction.

Mass Materials

The attention given to instructional material addressed to huge numbers grew out of the earlier days of fundamental education. It was then and still is an admirable emphasis. The enormity of the problems of illiteracy and ignorance and superstition called for an effort that could reach people by the millions. Greatness of need was supported by the availability of newer methods of mass communication. To the printing of ordinary books could be added picture texts with drawings and photographs and the use of the "comic book" type of cartoon to tell a serious story. Then projection slides, movies, radio, and television all added their particular contributions. The vistas of possibility open to a program of mass enlightenment seemed alluring.

Among the better examples are pamphlets for beginning adult readers published by the Pan American Union [27] on a host of subjects from pure milk to political history. Walt Disney has produced a series of cartoon films also for Latin American audiences on health and sanitation. The Department of Community Education on the Island of Puerto Rico [28] has made available both simple pamphlets and motion pictures of genuine merit and imagination. There are many others.

All these excellent materials have the limitation that they are addressed to man in the mass. No interaction between producer and learner is possible, unless the materials be used in connection with a

[27] Washington 25, D. C.
[28] Department of Public Instruction, Rio Piedras, P. R.

grouping of citizens that meets to compare differences in point of view, not as a substitute for educational experience that comes from personal contact with other learners and with a learning teacher.

Packaged Programs

When the citizen lives at a higher level of privilege, the adult educator who customarily deals with him will often seek to apply some packaged procedure. Such prepared programs will range all the way from instructions on how to persuade people to accept fluoridation of a city's water to outlines for reading and discussing The Great Books or The Great Ideas. This latter type of adult education, together with Liberal Arts for Adults, represents an appeal to a privileged minority selected from among the underprivileged. In such teaching, the benefit of growth toward freedom is limited to those who enjoy intellectual disputation. The concepts of freedom achieved are likely to remain at the verbal level.

There are many packaged programs. The constant temptation for the educator is to reduce his successful experience to a formula for universal application. All men tend to hope that they will find an easy "how to" method for solving their problems. Those packages which are most adequate are the outlines which allow adaptation to local peculiarities. The outline presented by Poston [29] is among the better packages. It is made out, however, for a relatively stable small American city whose citizens possess a modicum of town loyalty and formal education. A strict adherence to its use will rob the educator of flexibility to deal with other local needs.

Both mass material and packaged programs for smaller groups have their utility when they can be used as aids to growth processes inaugurated by citizens. A heavy or exclusive reliance upon them, however, bespeaks a determination to organize material for instruction rather than to find the experiences that can change lives. The attention is concentrated upon the information to be taught rather than upon people. According to this limited emphasis, a chosen community is made educative by inaugurating some instruction selected by a teacher who "knows" what people need.

The point of view of a redefined fundamental education is that a community becomes educative when people start to achieve a life together for themselves. The educational experiences occur as men

[29] Democracy is You, op. cit.

and women work cooperatively to perfect their common life. Educators expedite the growth of a community in order to expedite growth of its inhabitants. Many forms of instruction may appear but each is a side issue to developing citizens.

A New Creation

An educative community is something new for an age in flux. It is not the traditional community which was largely a place of unchanging conformity. It is not a geographic location upon a map with adult classes added. It is a group of people in a locality who work together to move toward an ideal of democratic progress. It has certain characteristics which are also goals of striving:

1. It is active. Citizens study, but for the purpose of guiding action intelligently and ethically. The promotion of cultural and intellectual projects may, however, be among the actions undertaken.

2. It begins with one group of people that devotes time and energy to some achievement for the common good. It grows further with other groups devoted to other such problems. Out of numerous group activities developed in the same area, involving often the same people, a sense of belonging together grows among citizens.

3. The membership of each group is voluntary. The ultimately achieved sense of belonging together is self-chosen.

4. Each group seeks to be all-inclusive, that is, it invites all factions, all points of view, every social level into membership. A true community endeavor benefits all, invites all into decision and control. Therefore:

5. It welcomes and encourages difference of opinion, developing skill to work together on practical problems without destroying the differences.

6. Each unit of action on a problem is small enough to allow personal participation in discussion and decision on the part of individuals.

7. The emerging community must be large enough to grant some control over important decisions that affect the lives of citizens.

The educative community is found not in being, but in becoming. A fundamental educator is not just a user of a community. He is an inspirer of those who will create a community of growth.

Educative use of the community calls for more than a definition that would satisfy the dictionary. It calls for a search for better human relations. It calls for helping people to discover, in their own lives, how to live constructively with one another. Because of the importance of ethical and intelligent human relationships, it becomes a magnificent research, on humble scale.

A Citizen's-Eye-View Typology

In helping citizens to create an educative community a start must be made with people wherever they are. For purposes of growth their geographic location is less important than their intellectual and emotional orientation. A major trouble is that, in modern times, so many have lost any loyalty to each other or to a place of residence. When people possess a diminished sense of belonging, the educator has less to work with. Nonetheless he must begin work with whatever accumulations of humanity lie within his chosen service area.

It is possible to present a classification of local atmospheres that are the beginning situations for growth from the citizen's-eye-view. One must realize, however, that any such classification necessarily oversimplifies, does some violence to details, and can never be complete. An atmosphere may describe the whole of a community or just some section of it.

Middle-Class General Betterment

Most American community experts operate with upper or middle-class citizens favorably disposed toward formal learning. They can safely assume that there is an existing hope of improvement to harness, some general religious good will, some self-confidence, and a modicum of familiarity with discussion procedures and parliamentary law. Assumed also are a reasonably comfortable standard of living, a minimum of mechanical contrivances, good communications in roads and newspapers and radios, good sanitation, and adherence to widely-accepted health practices. Granted that all these and some related assumptions are true, it is possible to offer a predetermined package of education that will usually represent some kind of progress. But even when all the assumptions are safely made, the supposedly universally-applicable formula should be used with care. For every community and every citizen is unique. And even middle-class units of humanity can vary from hamlets, to one-industry small cities, to rural or urban neighborhoods, to cities of many sizes. The yearning for educational formuli does not pay tribute to human similarity as much as to human love for packaged panaceas.

Unsolicited Need

Less often does the atmosphere of unsolicited need come to the attention of the community expert, even though such situations are more numerous. Citizens possess fewer of the advantages which were assumed above. The problem is not that of harnessing already-existing skills and enthusiasms. It is rather a question of slowly building up a hope that self-improvement is possible. That hope is the basis for an invitation to the educator. Much more skill is required and no packaged formula is useful; the reasons for lack of initiative are too diverse; the people must be approached with understanding sympathy, not with an outline. Often they have failed to identify any specific problems. As long as community developers are content to do no more than the easy job of serving the confident citizens of comfortable America they fall short of becoming fundamental educators.

Minority Civic Responsibility

Whenever a community, or a substantial portion of it, is committed to a program of general improvement, the course of citizen growth is easier to plot. But when the initiative comes from a clear-cut minority, a special problem of individual development is involved. Members of the minority frequently feel great loyalty to each other but regard other citizens as the unenlightened who must be won over.

The citizen progress sought is one thing for the eager promoter—it is another for the majority to be won over. The special interest promoters need to grow in sensitivity to their neighbors. The majority to be won over often lives in an atmosphere of:

Comfortable Indifference

There are people in any community who feel no need for personal growth or general betterment. They are steeped in an atmosphere of defensive immobility, wrapped up in their own individual worries. Though they have troubles, these are not interpreted to indicate need for change in themselves or in their community. They may put up a resistance of inaction and inattention to any local effort of improvement. They may be so numerous as to give an impression of comfortable indifference or smugness to an entire city.

Such people easily arouse frustrated emotion in the proponent of change. They cannot be dealt with sympathetically unless one understands the atmosphere of defensive indifference in which they live. The type of progress to be sought for them is an increase of sensitivity to the problems that worry their fellow men.

Righteous Conflict

An exaggerated form of minority civic responsibility is the situation of righteous conflict. The minority attacks entrenched evil and the comfortable indifference which allows it to flourish.

Here is a midwestern city torn into warring factions by a running battle between organized vice and crime and an embattled reform association. Without question the civic situation had required a clean-up for years. Gambling and violence have flourished, having a devastating effect upon youth and a corrupting influence upon municipal government. The reformers developed their vigorous campaign only after the situation had moved from bad to worse. But by their intransigent vigor they have managed to isolate themselves from many church members, the school people and other intellectual leaders, and even from honest political elements. Perhaps those who should have supported the crusade lacked the courage to take a possibly dangerous position. The anti-vice leaders became doubly courageous as a consequence, but split themselves away from fellow citizens. The local scene has become a battleground with three camps—organized crime in one, the flaming reformers in another, and the uncommitted majority somewhere in between.

Such campaigns are sometimes necessary in order to obtain a minimum of civic decency, in order to make individual growth possible. While such efforts do not create educative communities, they are often preliminary to utilizing a community for educative purposes. Zealots seek to attack and destroy an opposition. Educators recognize that an opposition, though wicked, is also made up of human beings with potentialities for growth. Some of the opponents may be destined for jail, but others can be rescued for development toward responsible citizenship. An educative use of such a situation of conflict is not easy to find. But it will be sought in positive action together for civic betterment of all who will cooperate, rather than in an effort limited to destruction of an enemy.

The fundamental educator should be wary about becoming involved in a campaign of attack. His function is constructive, positive. He welcomes the just and the unjust as long as they both will work for the general good.

Defense of Status

Vigorous promotion of reform sometimes produces a counter-pressure, an organized defense of things-as-they-are. The comfortably indifferent may move toward such an exaggerated resistance if they feel pushed too much.

Here is a southern state in which citizens have reacted against pressure to open schools to Negroes. They attribute their discomfort to interfering northerners and to Negroes who have forgotten "their place." They organize themselves into "Citizens Councils." This title, implying a general civic interest, is a misnomer. The purpose is to defend present privileges against change rather than to work for development. The membership is limited to those who believe themselves under attack. The attempt is to persuade a white majority to believe that they are victims, but to exclude the victims of their own discrimination. When "White Citizens Councils" become defensively inflexible they deny to their members the possibility of growth on one of the basic issues of the age.

Other pseudo-civic organizations can split a community into factions—tax-payers associations, patriotic societies that "prove" their loyalty by attacking people who accept other definitions of patriotism, and the like. The educator will be extremely wary of all such efforts. He will realize that the status defended is almost always one which is outmoded under the impact of changing times. The organizations can serve only to increase the kind of conflict that stultifies citizen development. In fact, progress for the promoters of such defensive associations is likely to be observed only as they give up their purposes. Progress for other citizens can occur as they ignore such special selfish pleading and move toward all-inclusive programs of improvement.

Conflict becomes creative only when the factions in dispute come together to discuss, understand, negotiate, and compromise. A community becomes educative not when it is used to enlist support for one side in a factional dispute, but when it is used to help all factions achieve mutually-respecting unity. Such a community of development is the local instrument for achieving a dynamic harmony between clashing races, social classes, religions, and political parties.

Community Stagnation

The town with a past but not much of a future has become a phenomenon of a dynamic industrial age. A settlement of people loses its economic basis for existence. Or too much comfortable indifference, or upper-class dictation, or even fruitless factionalism, all can contribute to community stagnation. Some such places become the "ghost towns" of America's former frontier, containing the decaying buildings of bygone usefulness with a handful of inhabitants. Others slowly lose population and purpose but continue to exist as accumulations of humanity with little vigor. The atmosphere of discouragement found in such places leads the energetic to flee and encourages those who remain behind to believe that "you can't get anywhere in this town."

Such locations are a special example of unsolicited need. The first development which the fundamental educator will seek is growth of the conviction that the home town has possibilities. There are many opportunities to be found. Their realization depends upon people learning how to work together, and not upon individual flight.

Boom Town

The boom town atmosphere, the opposite of that found in a stagnating center, is also characteristic of an industrial age. Such an atmosphere can be found in a new settlement built around an expanding factory or military camp, or in an old town which has rapidly burst its boundaries in order to serve such an installation. Sometimes the newcomers who flood in may be fellow nationals. Sometimes they come from an alien culture. Trailer homes or cheaply-built buildings may be observed, and often garish stores and other less legitimate commercial enterprises. But more important will be great dislocation of relatively rootless people, with fragments of families and people having little loyalty to the new (and sometimes temporary) location. There is little sense of belonging and little tradition to count upon. Traditions will be in rapid flux, often changing for the worse. There may be a high degree of public irresponsibility on the part of many inhabitants, even after months or even years of residence. Vice and crime may flourish and the forces of social control—churches, schools, welfare agencies, good government—may be at a loss to keep up with problems.

Such settlements of humanity are to be found all over the contemporary world. The first step for citizen development is to find a focus of loyalty that will pull together people who normally experience little sharing beyond common place of residence. It is necessary to find some such focus if people are to work together to release a creative cooperation commensurate with the material boom.

The Homeless

The homeless are dislocated folk who do not have even the hopeful lift of a boom town. Refugees are found in many parts of the world, the tragic human residue of wars and revolutions. In the United States are the equally tragic itinerant workers, with no permanent place of residence whose families follow the harvest and other agricultural activities through seasonal changes. Sometimes the homeless fit into the needs of rapidly expanding new industrial locations and thus take the first step on the long road to citizenship.[30] But in many nations there always seems to be a huge number who are surplus.

The finding of a home for the homeless is beyond the powers of the fundamental educator. He cannot solve that problem, but he can cooperate with others to work out a solution. The first necessity is obviously to find some spot of earth where these surplus people belong. The next is to discover some means by which they can support themselves with a modicum of decency. The educator can assist by helping to develop habits of cooperation and self-help, in temporary camps, and in more permanent homes when found.

The homeless will seldom request the help of community developers, though an invitation may come from interested friends. They must be sought out and patiently helped to reestablish a sense of belonging somewhere before progress toward citizenship can begin.

Endemic Despair

Millions of earth's people live in an atmosphere of endemic despair, not only the homeless but also great numbers who are firmly rooted in ancient hopelessness. Most are sunk in grinding poverty and ignorance; most suffer from superstitions which are incompatible with modern scientific thinking. But all possess a native tradition which must be respected. They are usually hampered by too great a subservience to authority and a lack of belief in their own ability to do things for themselves. They seldom will ask for help from educators, but they may be responsible for bloody revolutions if help is not made available. They too must be sought out if humanity is to progress toward democratic hopes.

---

[30] It was this that happened to the homeless celebrated in Steinbeck's famous novel, *The Grapes of Wrath*. The homeless become employees in West Coast war industries.

Their existing traditions, even though based on superstitions, must be modified only with their agreement. Their loyalty to village and tribal democracy may be utilized and enhanced. Their self-respect must be built up to become belief in their ability to help themselves. Beyond these generalizations, the progress of the citizen will vary enormously from one civilization to another. The fundamental educator must turn local tradition into assets for development, as he gradually introduces thinking from more developed parts of the world.

Community atmosphere is important for its effect upon the development of the citizen. The development will vary according to the prevailing social climate in which the citizen finds himself.

The citizen's awareness of the social atmosphere within which he lives is the starting point for development of an educative community. His ways of living, traditions, hopes, and fears are all elements which will give character to the emerging new creation of cooperation. Each educative community will be unique in its own way. There is room for an infinite variety that preprepared teaching aids should never be allowed to threaten.

Toward Variety

A fundamental educator starts operating with whatever location, size, and prevailing atmosphere is available in citizen experience. The prevailing atmosphere becomes gradually educative as a result of active, cooperative projects of improvement. In a democracy, policy is determined by majority vote, but atmosphere for citizen development is established by the minority which will take the lead. A negative atmosphere, dominated by self-seekers and the fearful, limits human growth potential. An educative atmosphere, dominated by those who grow through mutual trust, enhances it. In a vigorous community for growth, benefits extend even to those who are less active.

Assuming that a college has set up a program of fundamental education, how are good intentions narrowed down to a specific operation in a limited locale? The college:

1. Determines upon a service area.
2. Tries to locate within the area a locality with problems (a crossroads settlement, town, neighborhood, small city—preferably a section with a name).

3. Seeks contact with key figures who might introduce citizens to college people as potentially helpful friends.

4. Seeks to find local citizens who are worried about some problem. In conversation attempts to persuade them to believe that progress toward solution can be made, offering help from the college and other sources.

5. Encourages citizens to choose some local association, or form a new one, open to all, to work on this and other problems.

6. Sends students and faculty to meet, discuss, and work cooperatively with citizens as long as welcome.

7. Keeps teaching aids and academic wisdom on file to be used when helpful. Takes responsibility to persuade citizens to want the help the college can offer.

8. Expects other activities, addressed to other problems, to grow out of success within the group of first contact.

9. Expects to associate educationally with other groups, in the same locality, which will work on other areas of interest.

10. Expects to continue association with people in that locality over a period of years.

11. Hopes to observe growth of a general community spirit of togetherness with individual variety, out of the multiplicity of activities.

12. Assumes that there is no one single acceptable pattern for a good community, certainly not within different civilizations, and not even within the college's own domestic service area.

There is danger to democracy in seeking to find community in a definition that will satisfy historic or geographic criteria. Definition on either basis is likely to refer to a static association of men in an era when dynamic change is imperative. The fixed community of the past or present exerts a pressure toward fixed standards of belief and conduct. It could become the prototype for an enforced control of a dictator, a party-line, or a mass culture.

Educators imbued with a democratic hope will promote indefinitely developing local associations of men, based upon variety within, and variety from one association to another. They will seek the educational methods for citizens that will stimulate individual initiative while helping to raise standards.

The educative community is organized about an association of uniquely different individuals working together voluntarily for the common good.

Chapter IV

TEACHING METHODS FOR CITIZENS

Most educators will give verbal assent to the statement that man is a learning creature throughout life. It is only the *behavior* of teachers that belies the assent, limiting most of their effort to instruction in formal classes. Because of this behavior educational reformers have found it necessary again and again to call attention to basic purposes. Down through the centuries prophets have "discovered" that the development of the whole man toward his whole potentiality is the proper business of education.

Witness the example of Gandhi and his "New Education."

Gandhiji [Gandhi] defined Nai Talim, or New Education, as "Education for Life." "The field of Nai Talim," he said, "extends from the moment a child is conceived in the mother's womb to the moment of death."

But the definition "Education for Life" goes deeper. It refers not only to the span, but also the content and depth of the educational process. It means that education is both "for" and "through" life. "Education covers the entire field of life," Gandhiji said, "there is nothing in life, however small, which is not the concern of education."

The ultimate objective before this "New Education," however, is not only a balanced and harmonious individual life, but a balanced and harmonious society—in Gandhiji's words, "a juster social order in which there is no unnatural division between the 'haves' and the 'have-nots' and everybody is assured of a living wage and the right of freedom." [1]

As a latter-day prophet Gandhi has rediscovered age-old values which many practitioners of education have missed.

[1] From the Introduction to *Basic National Education*, p. v, Hindustani Talimi Sangh, Sevagram, Wardha, M.P.

64

THE STREAM OF LEARNING

The stream of learning which is the life of each individual tends to become stagnant when one has not been instructed in such basic skills as reading and simple arithmetic. It can become stagnant also when there is an assumption that learning has ceased because schooling has ended. The opportunity for educators who would contribute to mankind's progress lies in attention to the entire stream of learning, for whole populations. Gandhi's "New Education" is realistic. It should deal with "the entire field of life, for a balanced and harmonious society."

A school-centered educator can do no more than discipline learners' intellects or induce the acceptance of specific information or skills. A fundamental educator with vision cannot be satisfied with that small an influence. His ambition is to help learners redirect their whole lives toward self-chosen rising values.

All individuals are conscious of impulses toward both good and bad, within themselves. Throughout life they are subject to experiences that would encourage both. They can find satisfaction in following either. The educator who would be fundamental competes with myriad other influences. The closer he can come to the streams of learning in people's lives, the stronger will be his influence to help them achieve that self-direction which must be ethical if it is to be free.

INFLUENCING THE STREAM

There is no approved list of methods for teaching of citizens similar to that offered by textbooks in education for the young. Yet some methods can be pointed out. There are certain attitudes and ways of behaving to be recommended to teachers.

The most successful influencers do not look like professors or even teachers. They more closely resemble the learners, with certain differences that set them apart. For years good methods have been exemplified by missionaries who were more interested in people than in obtaining adherents to their own church, by social workers who could put aside the professional manner to deal simply with friends, by teachers who were persons in the community more than schoolmasters. The methods used cannot be listed for imitation, for they were unique to the user and to the trust he inspired.

A good example of domestic fundamental education is found in a project carried on by Flanner House, a social work center in Indianapolis. There many blocks of a former slum section are being rebuilt by a self-help, cooperative housing project. Residents of the slums who are to become owners of the new, adequate dwellings, pay their down payment on new homes by granting a designated number of hours of labor to the cooperative enterprise. They obtain decent places in which to live. But, more important, they grow in self-reliance and in ability to work together.

About three generations ago the British in India selected a few men to start a padlock-making business in an Indian city. The government's purpose was the production of needed equipment, but the result turned into the best of fundamental education. Over the years about half of the population of a city of 100,000 have become skilled craftsmen, operating a large number of small, independent plants. The whole character of a community and its inhabitants has been changed for the better.

In another Indian village a Scotsman started a small machine shop and foundry fifty years ago. By midcentury the founder had died but the small industry had been taken over by those he had trained, and had become a healthy business. Hundreds are employed at a new occupation which allows them a decent standard of living. Products are sold all over the nation and in other nations as well.[2]

Frank Pinder was an American agricultural teacher sent to work with the primitive farmers of Liberia under the "Point Four" program. Though a college graduate with experience as a teacher and as an economist for the Farm Security Administration in the United States, he did not look or act the role of the pedagogue. He lived on the land, with the people, often going about in a ragged white shirt, khaki pants and heavy work shoes. When coming to a village, he went immediately to the "palaver house" to talk matters over with the chief and others. He has persuaded native farmers to clean up swamps for the cultivation of rice, to plant hybrid corn and other vegetables, to improve their selection of chickens. He helped to modernize and expand the Liberian Department of Agriculture. While working with people where they live, he has suffered attacks of malaria, dysentery

[2] Both episodes from India are told by Arthur Morgan in an unpublished article, "The Effects of Adult Education Can Be Lasting."

and other tropical discomforts. But these are all accepted as a necessity of an effective educational process.

Pinder is not alone; there are many others going their quiet but effective way. Albion W. Patterson in Paraguay and Horace Holmes in India are carrying on similar programs. All these men serve under the United States State Department.[3] There are numerous workers in the field who step out of the academic life to influence the stream of growth for those who need their wisdom most. Usually these men and women fail to receive the plaudits that come to those who write the books in campus comfort.

Such devoted living with problems is scarcely open to either professors or students unless they take leaves of absence for prolonged periods. But contacts of shorter duration can be developed which will allow for at least partial entry into the lives of citizen learners. Educational effectiveness does not depend upon place of residence, clothes worn, or diseases suffered as much as upon the attitudes assumed by the educators and the way in which they are accepted by learners.

Group Learning

One village, within easy driving distance, became a locale for educational operation for a college bureau of fundamental education. Once a prosperous industrial and trading center, the town had been losing functions and inhabitants for a century. There was little employment in the village (men drove to work in distant factories); there was no bank, no telephone system, the school was overcrowded and in poor shape; no election for officers of the municipal government had been held in twenty-five years and the local public finances were disorganized. The college was invited to help by the town council. Professors agreed to do so but asked for a relationship that would last for a number of years. The long association was necessary to allow for the slow changes of an educational process, but also because no one was wise enough to offer immediate solutions to the multiplicity of problems.

The town board was disappointed when the association with the college did not grant immediate answers to pressing questions: how to finance equipment for a fire department; how to reorganize the municipal book-keeping; and so on. Instead the college asked for

[3] See *Point Four Pioneers*, Department of State Publication 4279, October 1951.

some problem of enough widespread interest to call out general support from the town and to allow students and faculty to work with citizens. After several weeks of apparently aimless discussion, an activity was selected—the rehabilitation of two small parks that had been overcome by the brambles of disuse. A committee, representative of the entire town, was formed. Members collected tools, lumber, paint, and seeds. College people came for several weekends of work with townspeople, cleaning out weeds, repairing and painting a bandstand, building picnic tables and barbecue fireplaces, installing drinking fountains, planting grass, flowers, and shrubs. But the most important outcomes were intangible, a beginning growth of local confidence in the ability to improve themselves, and an increase of friendship with college people. Professors, students, citizens, and their children worked together, ate together, sang and joked together, discussed the affairs of their town and of the world.

Once having concluded that the college representatives were people to be trusted, the acceptance has never wavered. New faces appear each semester; all are greeted as friends to be invited into both social affairs and serious discussions. Students and faculty feel free at all times to join in discussions, offering ideas for whatever a suggestion may be worth.

After the introductory activity of the park clean-up, interest died down. (Such a slump is a frequent occurrence in community projects in between episodes of vigorous activity.) For several months few meetings were held and no important activity was undertaken. At length citizens worked up their courage to face the great problem they wanted solved, yet feared the most—the inadequate school building. With encouragement from the college, they accepted the task of finding a solution. With a taxing power too small to support the cost of an adequate building, with complicated state requirements they did not fully understand, with decisions to be made on construction, land purchase, architecture, and engineering, the task was a formidable one. Starting with the park committee as a nucleus, a more permanent citizens' association was formed. It undertook to purchase land for the school board, to raise money by gift, and to erect a building that then might be deeded over to the school authorities. Discussion of the endless legal details, the study, the trips to county and state officials, the decisions that resulted in false starts that had to be corrected later, the money-raising ventures, all these details of self-education need not be recounted in full. Problem after problem was met, agonized over, and conquered. The promise of student help for certain phases of the work and the continued belief in the competence of citizens to solve problems, plus help in making contacts and in obtaining information, buoyed up the committee and the town. The continued interest of the college was manifested by numerous minor activities during the entire period; some students made historical studies of the town, others helped with children's recreation, helped to install playground equipment, and worked to tear down an old barn on the purchased property.

The school project continues (as do several other activities of general interest to community betterment). Ground will be broken for the new school building in a short time. There is not enough money in sight as yet, but the committee raises a little more each month. Though the way to ultimate success is not all charted, there is a resilient determination to carry on until the goal is achieved. As the treasurer of the committee has remarked, "We've just got to make this thing go."

From the point of view of group learning, the remarkable thing is the change that has occurred in the town's atmosphere within a brief period of approximately two years. When the college first came upon the scene there was a prevailing attitude of discouragement, the result of years of slow deterioration. Through action, study, discussion, self-criticism, and association with educators the atmosphere has changed to one of determined competence that doets not quail before setback or failure.

At one time, when the committee had raised more money in one evening than they thought possible, a professor warned them, "You are successful now and I congratulate you. But remember you will have setbacks. These enterprises never go smoothly. You will probably have a failure as discouraging as this evening has been triumphant."

Within a week the disappointment came. A piece of property they had hoped to buy at a nominal price was refused to them except at a figure beyond their means. Partly because of the warning, partly because of their own determination, they were able to reorganize their thinking and find a new piece of property that proved even better for their purposes. They expressed the belief that the professor was a prophet for anticipating the difficulty. In any case their growth toward responsibility included ability to accept disappointment and go on to accomplishment.

The scene can be shifted to a land foreign to midwestern American traditions. We have had opportunity to measure the educational skill of our college against the needs of one small conglomeration of the underprivileged, in a small valley in the mountains of Puerto Rico. Over a period of four years, with the later cooperation of the University of Puerto Rico, we have seen people rise to a high point of self-reliant responsibility. When we first arrived on the scene, they exhibited attitudes which accepted poverty, disease, isolation, and ignorance. In time they have achieved an organization which calmly and competently goes about the business of raising economic standards, improving farming practices and health, and meeting together to solve problems.

The list of the achievements of self-directed competence is impressive.[4] Originally these people had never known the experience of meeting together to talk over their problems. They went through periods of reluctance to "waste time" in meetings, several abortive attempts to set up an organization of officers and committees, beginning steps of the acceptance of small responsibility, and finally reached stages of increasing competence for larger and larger tasks. During this time the average family income has risen, partly because of an increase in the price of the chief crop, coffee, but also because the production of coffee per acre doubled, due to adoption of better agricultural practices. New homes have been constructed and others repaired; sanitary privies have been installed; both of these advancements have come about largely through the initiative of the people themselves. Monthly community meetings regularly bring out more than the officially chosen members of the community committee. Money is regularly raised by the people themselves, to erect a kitchen in connection with the newly-constructed school, or to build a new community and 4-H club building. The problems of these people have not been solved. But they are now aware of many of them and have developed a means for attacking them with expectation of making progress toward solution. In the process they have become new and stronger people, so much so that it is possible for the college to withdraw its intimate

[4] For full details see *A Pattern of Fundamental Education*, Eighth Annual Report of the Program of Community Dynamics, Earlham College, 1955.

stimulative contacts with the assurance that local people will go forward on their own initiative.

As in the preceding case, the college accepted responsibility only as a result of an invitation. There was a difference, however—the request for help was extended by the mayor of the nearby market town. His invitation was supported by a pledge of the Lion's Club of this town to support the enterprise. The inhabitants of the valley, sixty per cent illiterate and sunk in hopelessness, agreed to accept the collegians, but without much conviction that their promises of aid would be fulfilled. Professors and students agreed to become fundamental educators simultaneously for two levels of citizen learners, the underprivileged of an isolated valley and the upper-class privileged members of a service-social club. The first group acquiesced without enthusiasm or hope. The second agreed to go along, but with skepticism. The mayor and one or two members of the Lion's Club were convinced enough to encourage the college to move ahead. The initial responsibility for pushing the enterprise rested upon the college.

In this project the main device used at first was physical work. Students and professors came each summer to labor at whatever tasks local citizens chose. Every summer a work party came to sweat in the hot sun and to make friends with citizens who were gradually persuaded to join in. First a road was constructed, with tools and help from the mayor. Then a concrete-block school was erected. A few sanitary privies were installed, as an example which local people followed. Then a pole-barn community building was built. In each construction, citizens took more and more responsibility until finally, on their own initiative, they raised money for and completed a building for the use of 4-H clubs.

More formal educational activities appeared in community meetings, in recreation for children, in classes in literacy (for both children and adults), in clubs for mothers and fathers and youngsters, in instruction on nutrition, better farming, and child care. All such instruction came as a result of requests from learners. But students hiked through the whole valley to make friends with isolated and fearful families and to urge them to take advantage of the social and educational opportunities made available.

Much instructional material and personnel were brought to the enterprise by the University of Puerto Rico. This institution joined forces to bring students, later professors, and to assign extension workers. Motion pictures and simple pamphlets were used, as well as demonstrations of better practices. Citizens were instructed in home repairs, furniture-making, raising of rabbits for meat, and in many other skills. But the one attitude that made all the instruction possible was the trust and gratitude which local people felt toward the collegians who came to live and work among them for a time. The general attitude was voiced by one woman in response to an interview. "These college people are really crazy to come and work among us this way. But then, they are so nice about it that we have to cooperate. What else could we do?"

Methods for encouraging changes in group attitudes and behaviors can be described in more detail. The consumption of alcoholic beverages is a case in point. At the inception of the project, in consultation with upper-class supporters, it was decided that students and professors should refrain from drinking while in the camp which was part of the project each summer. This decision was reached in spite of, or because of, the prevailing habit of heavy drinking to be found among the very poor inhabitants of the valley. After discussion of the matter, successive groups of students themselves chose to remain abstainers from drink during this period of service, even though some of them came from homes in which social drinking was common. This decision was concurred in by the young people from the University of Puerto Rico when they joined the activities. Students and professors declined offers of drinks, explaining the group decision. No prohibition lectures were delivered, nor were the ties of friendship broken by condemnation. But the word spread about that these representatives of the college did not drink, though they were to be accepted as friends.

At the early community meetings a great many of the local people came intoxicated. Their competence to participate in the meetings was impaired. But, as time went on and the word spread that "this group does not drink," fewer and fewer citizens came to meetings under the influence of liquor. Later the drinkers attending meetings were the exception rather than the rule. Eventually citizens took over control and policing of meetings. They took it upon themselves to eject the one or two who came drunk or drinking. They explained quietly to visitors that private consumption of alcohol was the individual's own affair but that it was not proper at community gatherings. Any who chose to drink, therefore, must absent themselves from the meetings, even though they were still liked as persons.

Citizens of the valley have not become prohibitionists. The evidence is rather that responsibility for community progress took precedence over individual thirst. The change was not accomplished by direct instruction, but came as a result of a dawning awareness of the need for self-discipline. The general adoption of sanitary privies (provided free by the government) came by the same process of initiation, as did chlorinating of drinking water, improved conduct of meetings, a concept of the nobility of hard work, and many other more subtle changes.

A skeptical visiting social scientist, observing many changes that seemed almost miraculous, remarked, "All right, I will admit that remarkable progress has taken place. Was this due to the representatives of the college working here each summer? Can you prove that they deserve the credit?"

The chief Lion's Club supporter, a wholesale baker and man of great discernment, gave a reply which makes clear the essential methods used. "No, I can't prove that the college people did this. Who can determine cause and effect in such a complicated matter? But let me point out two things. First, changes did take place in this valley and in no other similar valley. And second, the changes took place after four hundred years of apathy and while the college people were hanging around."

"Well, I guess you win," said the social scientist. "Apparently these college people had some important influence. But I wish we could prove who did what."

Both his skepticism and his conclusion are commendable. The college people exerted an influence by "hanging around." The fact that, summer after summer, students and professors kept coming back to these people, was possibly a determining factor. The fact that the collegians came to share hardship and work, were friendly, did not come primarily to instruct, and were willing to learn, gave local citizens confidence to develop themselves.

The processes extended beyond the underprivileged in the little valley. The Lion's Club, which had been largely a social organization, raised money (over $4,000 in four years) and learned much of social responsibility. Various distant supporters and contributors came to accept a personal obligation for their own people, which was new to them. Governmental offices and agencies became interested and offered their support.

Perhaps the learnings found among citizens of the valley were no more significant than those occurring among more privileged people. Promoters of fundamental education among the underprivileged might give thought also to methods applicable to those higher on the economic scale. Perhaps educational work carried on for the benefit of the disadvantaged will succeed, in the long run, only as upper-class citizens learn to take responsibility for helping their own people.

Individual Learning

Individual learnings were achieved as parts of the group changes already described. The group is a composite of separate parts, but its atmosphere, in turn, influences development of all members. In the projects mentioned, new leaders emerged and became more responsible; individual citizens gained skills as discussants and as members of democratic assemblages; new habits, new autonomies, new values emerged.

A description of two additional modifications of individual streams of learning may prove instructive. Both were found within comfortable, middle-class, American communities. Both illustrate the interplay between external influence, group experience, and self-choosing.

A businessman was sent by his luncheon-service club to serve on a citywide committee for improvement of race relations. Out of obligation to his club, out of civic interest, perhaps out of a desire to side with the "underdog," he attended meetings faithfully. He associated with labor and management representatives, with church and school people he would not ordinarily meet, with delegates from other civic bodies, with members of racial groups that felt themselves victims of discrimination. After some time he made the remark, "You know, the problems in this field are much more complicated than I realized. I knew there were problems, but I had no idea they were so difficult."

With several others, he served as a member of a study committee that read books and collected information on the matter of better employment opportunities for racial and national minorities. College students and professors proved helpful in assembling and digesting much of this material. Later public meetings were held to encourage employment practices based upon merit, irrespective of race or creed.

The business man helped to promote these meetings, using his influence to invite other managers of industry to search their own consciences. When small delegations of employers quietly call upon their friends to urge fair play in allocating jobs and pay, he is available to join the persuasive party. He has not become a self-conscious evangel for righteousness. He has become an unobtrusive but most effective influence for that recognition of individual merit which is essential to a healthy democracy.

Max in an average American citizen, characteristic of his town and time. He is not especially interested in civic affairs. He is mainly concerned with his business, a restaurant.

Trouble arose for him as a result of a practice he held in common with other restaurateurs of his town. He sought out all manner of devices for refusing to serve Negro customers. Such discrimination was considered normal in the town's eating places, in spite of a state law which bars such practices.

Trouble erupted into an episode when some ethically overeager students from a nearby college decided to "do something about this injustice."

White students with colored friends "invaded" Max's restaurant, demanding service and waving copies of the state law in support of their demands. On the first occasion they were given service reluctantly. But when they attempted to repeat their triumph, Max, on advice of legal counsel, closed his restaurant for repairs and cleaning. Furthermore, he organized a mutual protective association of all restaurant managers to resist further pressure. This association was successful in delaying changes toward nondiscrimination over a period of several years. Through it, and through judicious use of newspapers, Max was able to build up considerable community support for the continuation of discrimination against Negroes.

About a year after this disastrous episode, the college set up a program of fundamental education. Among the enterprises slowly built up by the college program was a community council in Max's town. This council concerned itself with many problems of general welfare and improvement, better recreation and parks, traffic control and downtown parking, better business conditions for merchants, city planning, a church survey, and a host of other matters.

Among the items of discussion was discrimination against Negroes in privately-owned places of public service. Members of the council studied the matter, discussed possible solutions, but rejected the idea of pressuring their fellow citizens into better behavior. Instead they were quietly persuasive; they attempted to build up friendly contacts and a community spirit in favor of equal treatment for all, irrespective of race or religion.

Max was not a member of the community council, nor were any restaurant managers. He and they were at least mildly suspicious of the council but were aware of its deliberations. Some of its important members were friends and customers. Meanwhile the mutual protective association of restaurant-keepers languished for lack of threatening episodes to keep it alive. Its members came to have a more kindly attitude toward the college, since several of them became convinced that the institution was helping to protect them from further "attacks." Max was drawn into certain contacts and conversations which were more nearly representative of whole town welfare and not limited just to his business.

Students and professors were participants in various developments during this period of seeming quiescence, which continued some six years. The more impatient protested delay and insisted that something be done immediately to force an end to injustice. Reluctantly the overeager agreed to withhold their impulses toward direct action until the slower processes of change from within might be allowed to work. During the latter part of this period one restaurant, then another and another opened doors to Negroes without publicity. Students and professors took part in more than one conversation when a manager agreed to shift his policy to serve without discrimination.

Change finally came to Max as a result of another episode. Again students created an incident without faculty knowledge. In this case all were foreigners from lands in which the "race issue" has been exaggerated as a Communist means of condemning Western Civilization. Now, instead of seeking legal advice or resurrecting the protective association, Max appealed to the college and to the council for help. In conference with college people who were also active in the council, Max himself proposed to reverse his long-held position. The initiative for the decision came from him. He asked for the cooperation of professors in introducing small numbers of presentable and well-behaved colored people into his restaurant, a few at a time, then more and more. Especially he extended a welcoming invitation to the foreign students who had caused the disturbance, as long as they would "behave themselves." At last, with his willingness to learn new ideas his restaurant was opened to all customers. With this self-conversion of Max, who had been the greatest resister to non-discrimination, practically all other managers of eating places in the town have shifted policy. Max and others chose to change their values not as a result of group membership, but because of a shift in community atmosphere. The shift was brought about by a small, thoughtful, but active group.

Methods

The details of the processes by which people change have yet to be written. The methods by which educators influence associations and encourage experiences favorable to improvement, have yet to be described. Four general rules can be stated, however, even in the face of present ignorance.

1. If the educator assumes that men are flexible, this assumption helps to make them flexible.
2. To change men, change their experiences and the associations that provide the experiences.
3. If the educator wants men to move toward an ethical code that is good for all, he should help them to seek identity with all-inclusive associations which press toward the welfare of all. Experience with such associations of wholeness begins at the local community level.
4. If there is desire to help men control the objectives toward which, and the process by which, they change, they should be encouraged to form associations which they can control. The local community association has a great superiority over the national organization with a local chapter. The national bodies are not to be condemned, nor will they disappear. The educator will not oppose them, but he will be more interested in promoting those associations which give some local experience of autonomy and responsibility.

Although it is not yet possible to describe processes nor to give credit to those who "caused" changes, there is still some comfort for the venturesome educator and his students. The assurance is this: that if they will persist in friendly and cheerful contact with people, if they will press gently for the good of all, if they will remain calmly confident of people's ability to move toward the better, fundamental educators will frequently be witnesses of human beings in process of self-modification toward the better. What is more, they will find themselves praised for being "so helpful," when the main help they have offered is their interested presence. The praise should offer no occasion for self-congratulation. There will be failure and condemnation to balance against the favorable comments.

The Attitudes of Educators

The single most important method for fundamental education of citizens is the attitude of the educator. Teaching skill consists in adapting flexibly to the growth needs of learners. The good teacher attempts to bring together important elements of his own stream of learning with that of the people he serves. His skill, therefore, is found not so much in the proper use of techniques but in the kind of person he is, the kind of life he leads, his attitudes toward people and himself.

For professors and students these attitudes become goals of conscious striving. Professors must often work to perfect themselves over long time periods; their contacts with citizens are influential over a long time span. Change in student attitude need not require as prolonged an effort; being younger they are frequently more adaptable; they have less of a forbidding pedagogical manner to overcome; their mistakes have less serious consequences.

Identification with Learner

The most successful fundamental educators are those who come to live among and identify themselves with the people they would help. The Point Four Pioneers mentioned earlier are excellent examples. Technical instructors who live among less privileged people but insist upon maintaining their privileged status apart are less effective. Expert advisers sent to foreign nations who lodge in luxury hotels, ride out to villages in comfortable cars, and eat the food available only to the aristocracy seldom stir self-learning processes in the people to be helped.

Complete identification with someone else is not possible, however. No one can cease being himself to become part of the life of another people, especially if their standards are foreign to his own. The determining factor is not the amount of identification but the sincerity of concern. That concern should induce a teacher to abandon some of his own comfort, convenience, and demand for respect.

In one of our community projects in town S, students and professors were acutely conscious of lack of success. Citizens, as far as we could see, had achieved little. We attended meeting after meeting which proved to be frustrating. We offered recommendations but none were good enough to move the situation into important action.

One day, after months of dissatisfaction, a visitor from a neighboring town came in to our office to request help for his community. He was sure we could help him, he explained, because the citizens of S had told him how wonderfully helpful we had proved for them. This was the first indication to us that the people of S thought our efforts were productive. In further conversation with the visitor, it finally dawned upon us that although specific accomplishments were few, citizens were aware of learning processes which they credited to us. Two attitudes contributed to their gratitude, our willingness to continue meeting with them and the sincerity of our worry with them about their problems. Our conviction of failure had proved a key to success.

Citizen Initiative

By his attitudes and behavior an educator can discourage or encourage citizen initiative. When apathy is high and ideas for action few, when the teacher's own conscience tells him that he ought to be doing more than he is, when a "wrong" decision is being made or pursued, self-restraint in the teacher comes hard. It is difficult to determine when an educator should start something or should hold back. He must "play by ear," [5] an ear that is sensitive to the hope of citizen initiative.

In the Puerto Rican valley (as among many of the underdeveloped throughout the world) citizens were immobilized by their own despair, but also by inability to get together. They did not know how to conduct meetings, therefore could not arrive at decisions together. How then to stir cooperative self-help? Individuals could do no more than acquiesce in accepting ideas and labor from student work groups. But collegians could so conduct themselves as to invite an increasing responsible participation which would eventually allow them to withdraw.

By way of contrast, here is a community council made up of citi-

[5] A favorite comment of Jess Ogden of the Extension Division, University of Virginia.

zens, all of whom are college graduates and skilled in the conduct of democratic meetings. But they are handicapped by poor ability to understand or compromise a conflict between factions represented in the group. An educator, aware of the situation, having in mind a solution for the conflict, refrains from mentioning it for several meetings. He waits until he is convinced that members have begun to understand some of the differences of opinion that are pulling the community apart. He waits until members have begun to seek compromises between conflicting points of view. He hopes that someone else will propose a solution similar to the one he has in mind, to which he might add amendments. He offers his suggestion after several other proposals have been made and rejected. Then he offers his idea only as a possibility for consideration. He avoids getting into an argument between factions or about his proposal. The final decision must come from the group as a whole, not from his advocacy.

Credit for a good decision (or self-criticism for a bad one) goes back to the group as a whole. The educator is an adviser, not a decider. In a university graduate program that trains community educators, a student had to be dismissed from training. His instructors were unable to cure him of the habit of saying, when a citizen came forward with a bright idea, "Why, that is just what J. [a professor] has been saying all along." The statement may have been true but the point is one that an educator refrains from mentioning.

Too elaborate an array of equipment and supplies can prove a handicap when help is carried to underprivileged people. One of the advantages to be found in college community activity lies in the usual poverty of budget and equipment. When students and professors must obviously depend upon local people for beds and dishes, some food and entertainment, as well as tools and supplies for the activity, citizens begin to take responsibility.

In a college workcamp within a Latin-American setting, citizens concluded that students were poorly fed because they did not stop to have a mid-morning second breakfast. (Local people started the morning early with no more than a cup of coffee. Their solid meal came mid-morning.) They insisted upon the "starving" students sharing some of their food. Should the students accept? After talking the question over with native upper-class supporters the conclusion reached was affirmative. Citizens would have been insulted to have had their generously-offered food refused, even though they were themselves poorly fed. Students were urged, however, to accept small portions.

In connection with the same development project, professors begged equipment to be loaned to students. They also went out with teams of local upper-class sponsors to raise the money necessary to purchase tools and building supplies. One man of wealth, on being solicited, raised the question:

"I want to know, is this project religious?"

"Yes, it is. But we are nonsectarian. We are not trying to promote the interest of any church."

The potential donor cut him off. "Oh, I know you are not trying to win people over to your religion. But are you interested in people, in homes, in better families, in more intelligent parents, and in better-raised children?"

"That," said the professor, "is the heart and soul of the enterprise."

"Good. I will make out a check right now."

The money-raising committees, with true Latin-American deliberation, were too slow for the professor. He champed at the bit, wanting to go out with citizens each day. He returned to his college at the end of the work period, worried and frustrated that so little money had been raised. By the time he came back the following summer he found that the local committee had completed the task on its own initiative.

It is possible to be optimistic about the potentialities of people to grow beyond present limitation, provided the optimism is mixed with a judicious amount of pessimism. The educator needs a kindly, gentle, and cheerful cynicism that hopes for, but never predicts, the pro-social and responsible response in the other person.

The Ill-Defined Good

The fundamental educator needs to stand on the side of the general good in the eyes of citizens. The fact that the good is ill-defined is an asset rather than a liability. For the educator should not become identified with any particular school of reform, religious group, or political panacea. His attitudes should make it clear that he stands on the side of the general welfare of all people, but that he does not have a specific package of improvement to purvey. He is more interested

in helping citizens to grow toward their own improving concepts of
the good.

In the Puerto Rican project, a people who had been suspicious of
all outsiders for generations accepted the growth which collegians
inspired because these particular outsiders were identified as good.
Many of their ideas were peculiar according to local standards, but it
became clear that their intentions and general behavior supported
improvement which would benefit everyone.

The first community meeting ever to be held for free and open
discussion was called by the collegians. Citizens came to complain.
In speech after speech they berated everyone for their miseries—the
government, the church, the rich, everyone but students and professors. These they welcomed. Said one citizen in a typical burst of
Spanish eloquence, "We are so happy to have these angels come to
us through the 'Gates of Hell' [a locally-named small pass over a
ridge through which the new road was being built]."

In urging growth toward inter-racial harmony in a domestic community, college fundamental educators had difficulty in standing for
the general good. There was a tenseness of conflict between extremists.
Some fearful white citizens referred to collegians as "Nigger-lovers."
On the other side, some militant Negroes condemned the educators
because they would not fight for a noble cause, because they sought
to have white people change themselves toward justice.

One professor talked the matter over with the editor of the local
newspaper in the hope of obtaining adequate news coverage for joint
action enterprises. The editor took the position that discussion and
action together between races was undesirable. Better he said to "let
nature take its course" in such complicated problems.

He finally remarked, "Do you realize that you are playing with
dynamite?"

"Yes. But I have worked with explosive issues before. Just because
these matters are controversial and dangerous, we cannot stand aside
and deny people the benefit of intelligent and enlightened study."

"All right. As long as you realize what you are doing, we will support you in news columns."

"That is all we ask," said the professor. "That, and your critical
interest. We can make mistakes like anyone else."

In touching upon matters controversial, as a fundamental educator
does, he must discipline himself to avoid becoming a partisan. If he

becomes a flaming advocate of a political reform, he may find his usefulness curtailed by those name-calling slogans which are the stock-in-trade of politics. If he becomes religiously doctrinaire, he loses ability to reach those of different faiths. He must put his trust rather in the desirable educative outcomes of shared thinking together of every available point of view. He maintains his ability to promote such sharing by remaining the representative of an ill-defined good.

Arbitrary Separation

In college-administered fundamental education, it is not possible to separate teaching methods applicable to citizens from those useful for students. The two groups learn together, often in the same experience. Though the separation is arbitrary, there is justification for examining details of teaching practice for students.

The college fundamental educator attempts an exceedingly difficult but fruitful task, the merging of three distinct streams of learning for at least brief periods: the citizens' stream, that of students, and his own. The professor must be aware of all three, but in descending order of priority. Citizen learning comes first in his thinking because otherwise there would be no experience in community from which students might benefit. His own learning may prove as profound as any, but it comes as a result of serving the other two.

If methods, and spirit, and attitude are to spill over from one constituency of learners to the other, let it be from citizens to students, rather than the opposite. Though methods for students remain within the framework of campus discipline, they can profit by changes in emphasis that makes teaching more fundamental.

Chapter V

TEACHING METHODS FOR STUDENTS

If there is one conclusion upon which almost all college people will agree, it is this: a major, if not *the*, purpose of a college is the cultivation of the intellectual life. Is this purpose compatible with the emphasis upon problem-solving found in good fundamental education?

I suggest that we in colleges shall not gain the respect of society by deserting our chief reason for being, which is to persuade people in the community of the importance of knowledge. . . . action may be needed, since thought, insight, clarification are not enough by themselves. But if not enough, are they not basic and necessary? And are these not the primary functions of schools? [1]

May concentration upon community responsibility result in loss or weakening of the intellectual tradition?

Despite its liberal, socially constructive ardor, the "community approach" to adult education shows a narrow impatience with knowledge. Because it associates education with its search for obvious social benefits, it can pay little heed to scientific inquiries which have no known application to human services. But even where the social uses of knowledge are clearly indicated, its "education" will carry no more intellectual content than people need for the resolution of some immediate problem facing them. This type of education is not merely practical; it is in effect anti-intellectual. It seems to have but little confidence in the value of disinterested knowledge for adults, and prefers to leash adult education to the community's efforts to solve problems.

But if education and other communal activities are interrelated, it is

[1] Paul A. McGhee, Dean of General Education and Extension Services, New York University, "Adult Education and Community Action," *Adult Education,* Winter 1956, p. 80.

nevertheless true that they are separate and in certain respects independ-ent. It is possible to pursue the tasks of education without engaging in the affairs of community development.[2]

Such fears cannot be ignored or treated lightly. Colleges must re-main storehouses of wisdom, upholders of intellectual life and in-tegrity, and trainers of the more intelligent. Will the "community approach" jeopardize these aims?

Some of the fears refer to a limited type of adult education. When attention is concentrated upon nothing more than solution of an immediate difficulty, the effort will stimulate little intellectual growth. It is when successive experiences of problem-solving are used to en-courage long-term human development that an educational process becomes fundamental. The limited approach will be found in many universities which seek mainly to obtain proper care for the aging, or better sanitation and health conditions, or other immediate gains in communities. Its practitioners have little concept of the growth to-ward intellectual competence that is possible for ordinary men and women in an educative community. Their programs are seldom organ-ized about a concept of a life-long stream of learning for the indi-vidual and an age-long stream of development for the community.

Another fear cannot be dismissed so easily; the apprehension that freedom to investigate and think is hampered when tied to practical affairs. There are two schools of thought on the matter of preserving the intellectual life. One is isolationist; the other is applicationist. Both insist that theirs is the method for making intelligence vigorous. Both are right. Both should find their place in a college that lives in the modern world.

When adult citizen education is used to expedite student develop-ment, it tends to pass beyond the limitations of immediate problem or immediate community. The college attempts to help the student put his practical experience into a perspective of intellectual under-standing, related to theoretical study. This perspective carries back to citizens in further contacts between the two groups of learners.

It is necessary, however, to develop methods that go beyond many superficial activities that are acceptable as community outreach in many colleges. Classes that make community observations or inter-

---

[2] William Gruen, Associate Professor of Philosophy, New York University, "A Pragmatic Criticism of Community-Centered Adult Education," *Adult Edu-cation*, Winter 1956, pp. 86–87.

view citizens are not enough, nor are conferences that invite people in to talk about their problems. Apprentice assignments to necessary community functions are better but still fall short of an experience important enough to citizens to show a secondary benefit for students.

Methods for students are necessary which can touch them deeply. Experience must be offered to them which can come close to their streams of learning. By becoming involved in important processes of growth, by trying to understand and influence these processes within a perspective of intelligent understanding, they tend to bring the intellectual and the active into relationship.

The development of a disinterested intelligence is one of the greatest achievements of man. This historic development should be preserved by institutions of higher education. But colleges must not be satisfied to preserve; they must press on to new accomplishment as well. The achievement beyond is the making of intelligence available to man to solve his problems, to guide his growth.

Some Methods

Introduction and Invitation

Before any educational experiences can be developed in a community, the educator must be welcome. Some institutions attempt to invade communities at their own convenience. Then they inquire, with pathos, why people reject their offers of help. The communities immediately adjacent to a college campus may be antagonistic to the institution. A first obligation is to make the college acceptable. Because of old antagonisms, it may be wise to start first activities in some locality other than the immediate college town or neighborhood or city.

The college and its representatives are welcomed for a purpose, a multi-faceted purpose which goes beyond the normal activities of the public relations office. The citizen thinks of the purpose first as service to himself or his community, to help him solve some problems or make some progress that might not otherwise be feasible for him. The college agrees to help in offering service, may point out that students are ready, willing, and able to join with citizens to work on some needed improvement, or to be on call during a long period of gradual betterment. But the college must keep insisting that the reason for such service is the educational benefit that students gain in contact with citizens.

That is, the college lets it be known that a new and broader educational function is now available. It starts with service in response to community need, but presses toward more adequate learning for all people involved in the cooperative experiences that develop. The information can be spread by various means—newspapers, radio, through speeches to churches and clubs. But the most convincing publicity comes from the development of a successful project of actual work in a community or two. Then the word spreads from person to person.

No better method for obtaining an invitation to start the first project can be offered other than the building up of friendship with an increasing number of people in the chosen service area. The selection of the people who might prove most receptive is a matter peculiar to each institution and probably also to each professor. Sometimes the approach is through alumni, sometimes through ministers of churches, sometimes through local chambers of commerce or service clubs, or through those who have a general interest in public welfare. Some faculty person, or more than one, must spend time in circulating about, talking to people. Supporters thus cultivated can provide interpretation in communities, can often give leads on service opportunities, but most important of all, can suggest to citizens that an invitation to the college will probably elicit a positive response.

After successful or even partially successful completion of two or three projects of community help, invitations will begin to increase beyond capacity to meet them. There then can be some choice on the part of the college. But there will always be need for the contact with sympathetic supporters to provide a means for choosing projects and to open the way for encouragement of invitations which do not come spontaneously.

Maintaining Acceptance

Once a college's reputation for service-educational activities has begun to grow, some faculty representatives must take responsibility for continuing cordial relations. Such contact occurs best off-campus and casually. The faculty members travel about the service area, "dropping in" on people, talking with them formally and informally, expressing interest in their problems and in their progress. This contact work needs to be looked upon as a legitimate expenditure of a professor's time. The time is indeed being spent upon teaching; each conversation, telephone call, letter, and speech may have such a function. And if, as is often desirable, a student or two accompanies a professor in his contact work, there is material discovered of educational benefit to the young people. Experiences with community personalities and situations can be reported to classes for analysis in pursuit of understanding.

Visiting, though seemingly casual, can be planned and systematic. Beyond the keeping in contact with sympathetic supporters, there is the opportunity to build up an awareness of the life which is normal to the college's service area. After listening to people tell of local problems, it is sometimes possible to attend meetings where these matters are discussed. The professor and his students can become familiar with the characteristic organizations that are to be found in an area, with the kind of people who are members, and with the kind of difficulties that engage their attention. Out of such contacts can be developed a cordiality of relationship which will allow the college to become associated with various significant local groups, when it does get around to helping citizens to work on their own problems. Comparative studies of different settlements of people become possible. At first such studies may be superficial, when based only upon casual visits. But first impressionistic records kept allow selection to be made later for more intensive research studies.

As he visits, the educator begins to perfect a device which is essential to all fundamental education—friendship. Obviously the friendship must be genuine. It is an end of the whole effort. It must grow out of a bona fide concern for the welfare and uniqueness of the other person. But it is capable of conscious cultivation when the educator seeks to discipline his own attitudes.

Colleges that accept community responsibility will find that they are often solicited for advice from citizens whose situation is relatively unknown to them. A community improvement association of one town has come to a college for approval of a letter to be sent to all citizens on a survey questionnaire, without having invited college people to attend the meetings that drew up the documents. The knowledge of local facts that would make intelligent comment possible can come only from intimate contacts. Professors need to shift their role to that of friend. Students can prove enormously useful in bringing about such a shift. Their cheerful informality can open doors to a college. And in the process, students learn how to collect and organize information that is to be recorded and related to general theory in classes.

Observation and Recording

When there is concern for the welfare and dignity of the person observed, when he is a participant at least to the extent that he begins to understand and sympathize with the educator's purpose, then there need be no violation of friendship, either in the observation or in the keeping of records.

One of the elements of disinterested intelligence is the ability to be objective. It is easy to achieve objectivity about someone who is far away, either geographically or emotionally. The achievement of the attitude becomes more difficult as the observer shares the purposes and worries of his subject. College students can be wonderfully objective about citizens in a community, especially when they see them for the first time. But when it comes to describing their own compatriots on campus (or themselves) they may lose this disinterested attitude.

Many colleges have had experience with objective contact that denies friendliness. Students on "field trips" observe and write descriptions of that which they have seen. They tend to stand on the sidelines as nonparticipant and nonsympathetic observers. Or they may make surveys of delinquency or bad housing as part of a class assignment. Again they can display a noble indifference. Or conversely, their hearts may bleed for the unhappiness and injustice they see. In neither case have they achieved an attitude which would allow intelligence to contribute substantially to solution of the problems they encounter. The need is to describe those who are intimate friends with accuracy and, at the same time, to spread the circle of understanding friendship.

Some colleges that accept a community obligation have mixed students and citizens together in cooperative self-surveys. The participation of citizens may range all the way from an authorization for the students to proceed with the work on their own to an actual laboring together in meetings, to tramping the streets and ringing doorbells, and to the adding up of results together. The more time students and citizens spend together on a common enterprise, the better friendship develops and the better is objectivity achieved.

When students write reports of shared experiences, these become raw material for educational processing. Such accounts should be brought into the discussion of a classroom for analysis and critical thinking. It is thus that the tendency to make emotional judgments is discouraged and an ideal of objective accuracy built up.

Does the freedom of students to discuss their elders become violative of friendship? Not necessarily: it all depends upon how the friendship is maintained. Citizens are told, "Of course the students keep records. Of course they discuss the things they see. Of course they learn from citizens they associate with. That is the only pay they ask for their help, the chance to become better citizens themselves by learning from their elders who are struggling with the real problems of life." The teacher sets the tone of student discussion, he mildly modifies condemnation, turning criticism into understanding. Often the tendency which a hasty student dislikes is the very characteristic that makes a person unique and interesting. The opportunity to find value in variety of personality arises when discussion sharpens awareness of difference. Eventually some citizens are invited to join in the classroom discussion. Such an occasion allows the citizen to develop his sense of humor and the students to cultivate tact.

Observation and descriptive recording represent a good beginning. As educational devices they contribute to cultivation of friendly objectivity. But more active experiences are necessary to complete the story. How does one move from description of that which is, to promotion of that which ought to be?

Work Periods

In contemporary college practice, nonclassroom work can refer to many kinds of activity in the regular job with pay, the job responsibility without pay, and the experience of voluntary group labor. The first we will refer to as individual work assignment, the second as apprenticeship. The third we will designate as a work period.

Regular work assignments have appeared in many colleges as a part of the curriculum. The most widely known is the Antioch Plan of Cooperative Education, though such programs are to be found in other liberal arts institutions and in engineering and business schools. Such plans have major educational justifications, but these are primarily of a vocational nature. Because they are poorly coordinated with the scholarship of general education, they contribute little to the preservation or application of the intellectual life. When co-ordinated, their focus of interest tends to concentrate attention upon success in the student's future career. Contacts with citizens do not utilize the full gamut of community experience or of human problem.

Apprenticeship has a long history outside of schools as well as in them. It appears as internship for such professions as medicine and nursing. It has developed also in the work of general colleges. Such work experience is to be found in the routine maintenance of community functions. Although such activities give little experience of community development, they familiarize students with the housekeeping chores of citizenship. Alone they have limited educative value. A student accepts an assignment as a Sunday School teacher or Boy Scout leader or substitute minister in a church, as a director of a recreation program, as a worker in a hospital, as a practice teacher. Such responsibilities are normally carried on without pay, for "experience."

If the college offers counseling to the student as the work goes forward, and seeks to utilize the experience for educational discussion, the keeping of records, reporting, and critical analysis of experience in a group can turn drudgery into valuable education.

As educational devices, work periods can vary all the way from thoughtless exercise to physical labor which is an integral part of an intelligently-guided process of community growth. Though the leg-work type of labor be low in the scale of educational merit, it should not be discarded as a device for gaining genuine interest in community activity.

Work periods can be developed for a wide variety of activities. A church survey of an entire city put teams of students and citizens out ringing doorbells and interviewing householders together over many Sunday afternoons. One day a student from a Near-East Islamic nation went interviewing with a member from a Southern Baptist church. After the day's work a professor asked the citizen what he thought of the experience.

"You know, this is the first time I ever saw anybody who wasn't a Christian."

"How did you get along with him?"

"Oh fine."

"What did you talk about?"

"We talked about God."

"And what conclusion did you reach?"

"We decided that we both had about the same idea."

The student, on being questioned about the citizen, remarked, "Oh, he was a good fellow. I learned a lot from him."

There is no evidence that the Baptist was converted to Islam or the Mohammedan to Christianity. There was evidence of that increase of sympathetic understanding which is necessary to useful wisdom.

Another work period was devoted to cleaning up the neglected home of a retired school teacher, others to repairing homes in the slum sections of cities, others to building an old people's home. Still other periods found students conducting surveys and adding up results in company with citizens. At other times, recreation programs for youth and adults were carried on. The possibilities are endless. The planning is cooperative. The execution brings students and citizens together in common effort.

The most elaborate organization of a work period is found in a workcamp. So important is this activity that the next chapter is devoted in entirety to such experience.

If work ennobles, it is work with meaning and purpose that educates. Students, citizens and even educators have been known to prefer the routine of continued work rather than the disquiet of fundamental thinking together about their work. Experience, even that which is vigorous and exciting, can be miseducative unless it is digested in interpretive discussion.

Participation in Planning

In order to lift work experience above the level of muscle-stretching or shuffling-of-files, it is necessary that the worker be a participant in planning.

This experience is best found in attendance at meetings of community councils and committees. There students have a chance to observe and take part in the slow and often fumbling processes of local democracy-in-action. Students can then come to understand that the slow and often repetitive talk they participate in embodies several simultaneous processes of growth: community progress toward unity and improvement, citizen maturation toward tolerance and discussional skill, their own growth toward understanding and patience. They are urged beyond impatience to awareness and study of human developmental processes.

An Oriental student in attendance at our college was present in several community meetings as part of his undergraduate study. In subsequent class discussion he offered the opinion that "Americans talk too much. They just talk and talk and never seem to get anything settled." A month or so later, after continued attendance at meetings and discussions thereof, he stated himself differently, "I have changed my mind about Americans' talking."

"Do you mean you no longer think they talk too much?"

"Oh, I still think they talk a lot, but now I see why. They talk to convince each other, to think things through, to agree so that they can act. This is the way democracy works.

"Now in my country nobody would have the patience to talk that much. Or if they disagreed with each other as much as Americans do, they would start a fight among themselves. My people do not think out loud the way Americans do. They expect to have someone tell them the correct thing to do. Americans talk a lot. But I think now it's a good thing."

The fact that students may put up a temporary resistance of boredom to attendance at many meetings should not discourage the fundamental educator. The teacher invites and urges interest. He expects students to discover that successful democratic citizenship is more than a matter of enthusiasm for freedom. They often find that good citizenship involves careful thinking as a guide to action.

Disciplined student thinking becomes a part of participation in meetings and in the on-campus discussion that occurs before and after attendance. This pre- and post-analysis of contacts occurs in classes or seminars or informal conferences. These discussion opportunities allow the teacher to stir interest in, and give meaning to, the learning processes of democratic thinking in which the student has taken part. In them also can occur analysis of practical application of theoretical wisdom, in response to discovered community need. Students and townspeople together move from discussion of problems, to study, to decision on a plan, to joint work periods, and finally to judgment upon both the planning and the work. When the educational procedure is functioning at its best, the ability of students to analyze the process in classroom carries over to meeting in community.

In time, with some aid from the educator, the citizen also develops a little more objective awareness of the processes of growth through which he moves.

Study of Community Development

Ordinarily, intensive study of community development would seem to be a responsibility for a graduate school. Probably the major burden of research in such matters belongs within the graduate work of a university. But a liberal arts college can make an important contribution of process-description and record-keeping. Where it has a few graduate students, it can analyze some data and develop some understanding of theory. In any case, a college can gear into the research efforts of a university when a cooperative relationship has been set up between the two institutions.

In making observations and in collecting records of growth for intimate studies of community development, small colleges have a distinct advantage over larger sister institutions. Their location is usually so distributed geographically that each may enjoy an undisputed service area. Within that territory it is possible for a college to cultivate a cordiality of friendship with people in many localities. The university researcher has better facilities and more specialized training at his disposal. The smaller center can collect data and interpretations by associating with people in relatively relaxed, natural situations. A cooperating university can collect such records from many smaller institutions. It can formulate general conclusions which grow out of numerous local examples of community development.

It is easy for a small college to neglect intensive studies even when it carries on a community program. Its budgetary allotments may be directed mainly toward teaching (traditionally defined) of undergraduates, formal adult courses, and service projects. Professors and college authorities may fail to recognize the opportunity that lies in intimate study of community growth processes. The opportunity becomes available only when one or more selected localities are chosen for concentrated attention over a period of several years, when careful records of every contact and change are kept, when students and professors try to understand and even predict the stages of development in which they are participant observers.

The Role of the Outsider

Although the educator and his students succeed in being friends to citizens, although they seek to identify themselves with community thinking, they inevitably remain outsiders. The collegians are campus-oriented. The citizens are community-oriented. The collegians as fundamental educators should attend meetings, take part in discussion, help in work. But they should not vote when decisions are finally made or officers selected. It is better that they do not accept election as officers themselves, or otherwise relieve local people of the responsibility for local development. They may serve on community committees, but as advisers that share work. It helps, too, if fundamental educators can make clear that, though they are deeply interested in the welfare of the immediate community, they are interested also in general developmental processes elsewhere.

It is well that a college fundamental educator remain a helpful outsider. Even when he becomes a resident in a community, local citizens are aware that he was not born there, comes from some other culture or social level, has loyalties elsewhere, and probably will move on to another scene of operations in time. Since representatives of a college can never deny their institutional connection, they had best utilize it to help stimulate local development.

Their greater interest in matters intellectual will always designate the collegians as outsiders. They may as well live up to their expected role by raising questions that call for deeper study, more thorough-going thought. It is possible to press for more profound thinking, for wider wisdom, for higher standards, without being patronizing. To learn how to do so as a friend should be one of the aims of a liberalizing education.

The Undergraduate Emphasis

Educators must be aware of the needs of both undergraduates and graduates. Formal higher education usually separates graduates from their less mature compatriots. Such is the nature of community development, however, that learners at various levels of maturity benefit by interaction with all other learners. Though many phases of the enterprise of higher education may be integrated in a single community experience, it is the obligation of the educator to separate out different emphases to help learners of different levels.

The Citizen in Training

For the undergraduate, the emphasis is upon the training-through-experience of future citizens. This stress is part of the liberal arts responsibility of the college.

Does citizenship training in community context provide an integration of all of liberal arts education? Not at all. There are many cultural treasures which should be taught whether immediately practical or not. To the extent that these represent eternal verities, however, they should be applicable to every historic era, even to the uncertainties of the present confused age.

Is the emphasis upon citizenship training in community all of citizenship? Not at all. There are facts to be learned, appreciations and values to be examined beyond any immediate experience. Community contacts provide a beginning of concreteness for citizenship training. The educator who can accept the challenge points out that the concrete application either illustrates or falls short of abstract theory, and why. He then goes on beyond the observed limitations of any specific experience to seek the broader principle, the more universal fact.

Should this emphasis upon citizen training be limited to a liberalizing education solely? Not at all. There are other roads to citizenship responsibility. Undergraduates from a school of agriculture or engineering, or education, or nursing, or from any other school which trains young people for a paying job, should be trained for responsible freedom. To raise their eyes from mere job interest to citizen enthusiasm is to introduce a liberal arts emphasis into vocational education.

Fitting into a Curriculum

It would be possible to introduce a curriculum of requirements, adding up of credits and grade point averages, and conferring of degrees. Such lock-stepping of events which should become vital experiences for the undergraduate would destroy the spirit the device was meant to serve. Yet to classify them as extracurricular is to deny them a recognition of legitimate acceptance within the basic purposes of the institution.

If the curriculum be defined as the totality of experiences made available to undergraduates, the college offers a wide variety of activities, intellectual and social, academic and athletic, quiet and active, theoretical and practical. Some activities are more interesting, some less; some earn credits recorded in the registrar's office, others have more intrinsic rewards. Some are compulsory for all students, some for particular certifications of skill, and others are open to free selection.

The education acquired by any one student is a mosaic of selected experiences, no two patterns being the same. The balance between compulsion and free choice for students is one which must be determined by every institution. But the faculty's obligation to students is not discharged when that balance refers only to courses listed in the catalogue. Professors must think of the total curriculum of all experiences and be prepared to guide as well as compel. Perhaps in the long run the encouraging into noncredited and noncompulsory activity is the most important part of any student's education. For in these activities his learning is urged on by the motive power of his own decision.

The experiences provided by the devices mentioned can be found in both the academic and the experiential part of the curriculum. Some simpler experiences can be included as parts of courses in the social sciences, psychology, and education. Beyond these the college may want to set up separate courses, to provide discussion-study centers for community outreach, such as a Seminar in Community Development, or in Fundamental Education, or in Social Action-Research. But many work periods and most workcamps belong outside such formality, though they are an important part of the total curriculum.

When faculties can broaden their definition of curriculum to include formal and informal experiences that make for citizenship, they can arrange devices in a graduated sequence. Such a sequence is implied roughly, in the order in which we listed devices. In an advancing complication of skills and understandings, students find themselves invited and welcomed into more and more complex forms of training. When students reach certain levels of sophistication, faculty advisers urge them into the proper activities. And other faculty members plan to utilize in their own courses the new insights and appreciations growing out of the activities. But when guiding into citizen experience, advisers should not feel bound by even the compulsion of an agreed-upon sequence. The volunteer enthusiasm of the individual is more important than any formal order of prerequisites.

A careful examination of the college devices that contribute to citizen development can make clear that indulgence in fundamental education will support and enliven undergraduate liberal arts instruction. But the final proof of compatibility will come to many colleges only as they, themselves, become involved in educational processes addressed to modern man's fundamental problems.

GRADUATE EMPHASIS

Most universities have programs of adult education, extension work, or continuing education, or special institutes for business men, farmers, traffic experts, or women's clubs. These special services can proliferate endlessly. They are found in greatest abundance within the tax-supported institutions which must, perforce, respond to demands from citizen groups. They are usually organized at the graduate level, sometimes offering training for specialists in a particular field, sometimes offering no more than the service requested by citizens.

These special services represent a limited type of community education. The service remains out on the periphery of the curriculum, offering no benefit to undergraduates or to the faculty as a whole. The central liberalizing purpose of the university's own general college remains untouched by contact with citizen growth.

American higher education has tended also to separate the undergraduate from graduate levels, on a university campus and from one institution to another. A liberal education is found in a college. A professional education is found in a university with a populous graduate school. Such a separation is necessary for many highly-trained fields of specialized knowledge. But the field of professional community education (also requiring great skill) gives opportunity for closing this educational gap. The graduate training of community fundamental educators can be carried on most expeditiously in contact with undergraduates.

Every college with a community program should not necessarily set up a separate graduate program. Few of the smaller institutions could afford to institute an independent high-level professional training in this field. Their main reliance must be placed upon the more extensive facilities of universities. A cooperative relationship between a university and a number of smaller institutions would open the way for graduate students to spend part of their time on field assignments with the undergraduates of cooperating colleges.

The graduate emphasis for fundamental education is upon professional training of community educators, in contrast with citizen training for undergraduates. This professional work belongs, for the most part, in universities. A few better-equipped colleges can enter the field of graduate work, to supply a part of the variety.

The trend in graduate schools is away from the adding up of credit hours from courses and toward the crediting of any genuinely educative experiences. Credit should be granted for passing certain courses, but it should be allowed also for working contacts with citizens in communities, when these contacts are digested educationally. One kind of experience worthy of such credit is the dealing with undergraduates active in community, students who are citizens-in-the-making. In addition, each graduate student should be expected to make his own individual research contribution in a narrower field, so that he could be presented to possible employers as one peculiarly qualified.

Research Attitude

The cultivation of a research-experimental attitude toward all human situations is important in the fundamental educator. Too many graduate students have been trained to place reliance upon some single approved procedure in dealing with human ills. They have not gained the humility to recognize that neither they (nor their professors) have quickly applicable answers to the practical problems that worry people. The answers must be sought by the people involved, with some help and guidance from educators like himself.

There are difficulties involved in using the words "research" or "experimentation." To the purists, these refer to some specific project undertaken by an investigator, with dates for beginning and termination, with a scholarly monograph resulting, all complete with footnotes and bibliography. Such a written production is necessary in the training of a fundamental educator as evidence of certain maturation. But more important is the achievement of a research attitude of continuing search for the true and the better in people.

Wise humility will allow the fundamental educator gradually to enlist the cooperation of the citizen in some research activities. The research attitude should become contagious. The citizen needs to look upon himself as an object for his own experimental thinking and action, not merely as a subject for investigation by someone else. The graduate student can begin a spreading of the research attitude toward other people by working toward this end in his supervision of undergraduates.

The Avoidance of Expertness

Trained fundamental educators must become experts in human relations. But skill in this field can remain humble. It is the expertness that parades itself in answer to questions about specific problems that needs to be avoided. Even in graduate school the fundamental-educator-to-be needs to say, "I don't know. But I can help you to get the necessary information." It is wiser for him to maintain his amateur status with his co-learners in community than to appear overwise.

The fundamental educator is an expert in processes of the whole. And he attempts to remain as near as possible on the level of the citizens he deals with.

THE RECAPTURE OF THE PERSONAL TOUCH

The educational methods used in community are based upon interest in persons. Those used on the campus could recapture more of the personal touch.

Admiration for the Intimate

All of contemporary higher education suffers from over-admiration for gigantism. Perhaps the university can be forgiven in some measure, because it makes a virtue of necessity. But neither it nor the independent college should be content to provide no more than mass instruction.

Intimate personal concern for the welfare of students can easily turn into the coddling of the weak. How is it possible to be genuinely concerned about the progress of individuals without yielding to a deterioration of standards? When community activities are undertaken, the interest is not limited to students; they are asked to focus their interest upon others whose need is more obvious than their own. The concern for persons is directed outward, away from self.

Family Atmosphere

In the early days of most American colleges and universities a greater concern for each student prevailed because a family-type atmosphere was more common. Such an atmosphere could be reestablished in small institutions and large. The family is the first social situation that encourages growth of personality; some extension of its spirit into more formal education is possible.

Several devices listed provide an opportunity for developing an adaptation of family atmosphere in some aspects of college work.

Every institution of higher education possesses an unused asset for creating a family atmosphere: most of the instructors are married. Commonly only one member of the marriage partnership will be employed or utilized by the institution, usually the male. His wife is usually not called upon for educational services, especially if pay is involved, lest there be accusation of "nepotism." Consequently many wives, often well enough educated to be real educational assets, are denied opportunity to make contributions that would benefit both student and college.

In certain college devices contributing to fundamental education a huband-wife combination is almost indispensable to the adequate emphasizing of personality values. It is possible for a college to enlist the services of the normally non-participating marriage partner to complete a team, in certain situations and for limited time periods. Such an institutional course of action is possible, with expenses paid and possibly with a little compensation, without violating too much any sacred tradition against husband and wife working together.[3]

At two points the husband-wife team is important to college fundamental education. The first is the effect upon the community. The second is the effect upon the students.

In every human settlement with potentialities for development, there will be found both masculine and feminine interests. Good fundamental education will call for representation of both on the team of educators that hopes to help people. In a village of the underprivileged, masculine and feminine roles will often be sharply differentiated. A man who attempts to meet village wives in homes or to converse with them about problems of child care will find himself handicapped. Conversely, a woman will frequently not be ac-

[3] There are some notable and exceptional examples of husband-wife employment by the same educational institution. Often the two must be separated into unrelated departments, lest they offend some rule. In a few instances they may work together in the same program. One of the most successful community operations in the U.S.A. is carried on by a husband-wife team, Jess and Jean Ogden at the University of Virginia. Other institutions could study their activities and writings with profit.

cepted by the village males. In a privileged and better educated social setting, there will be found both male and female organizations whose interest and enthusiasm must be enlisted for community progress. A better and more rapid job of citizen education is possible when both sexes are represented among the educators.

When unmarried male and female members of an educational team appear upon the community scene, especially if they are to be in residence for a time, uncomfortable questions are often asked and scandalous answers may be circulated, even though their relationships are actually above reproach. This tendency to ascribe immoral conduct to members of a team from a college can prove detrimental to the whole enterprise, especially when educators are operating among people whose place of residence or standards are foreign to them.

Among students also, it is important to provide an example of a healthy atmosphere between a husband and wife. Work parties that go off-campus into community should under most circumstances include both male and female students; the presence of both sexes, working hard together, is beneficial to both citizens and students. Often a work party will be away from campus for long periods, at odd hours, or overnight, to be in residence on the job. Though chaperonage in the mid-Victorian sense is no longer acceptable to students, it is important to provide a norm of conduct for young people which will help them to move toward happy marital adjustments.

For both citizen and student to work with educators who exemplify desirable relationships between male and female is to contribute to educational progress of individuals both in community and on campus.

The Useful Intellect

The methods discussed do not indicate the full gamut of possibility. Colleges entering the field of fundamental education must be prepared to experiment imaginatively. No college yet does more than feel its way toward educating students by making its intellectual treasures available to all men.

The intellectual life cannot psychologically, and must not morally, be divorced from the whole of living. No one should expect it to be vigorous and healthy in complete isolation. It will survive by its own integrity but also by its adaptability to serve.

There are two forces of the contemporary world with which the defenders of the intellectual tradition in college must contend. These are:

The long-time trend in higher education toward the enrolling of a majority of youth and toward the teaching to them of "practical" learnings. The problem is to serve the increased proportion of the population, yet maintain the excellence of top-flight education for the intellectually elite. The exploration for answers should move away from mass teaching toward fitting instruction into the streams of learning of individual students. It moves also toward exploration of methods that use practical experience to stimulate thought about and study of the theoretical, in a context of wholeness. Community outreach into fundamental education opens up such possibilities.

The desperate need of humanity for intelligent guidance that honors cultural appreciations and ethical values. The men and women and institutions that preserve the intellectual life which could guide cannot, in conscience, keep their wisdom to themselves. But their obligation goes beyond trumpeting information to those who "should" welcome it. They are obligated to explore methods for making the intellectual tradition useful. If students become partners in exploration, the whole of higher education will be improved.

There is no easy answer to these two forces of modern times. A bold examination of the methods of college fundamental education will provide one range of answers. The methods that seem promising are those which stimulate each student to find his own balance between the theoretical and the active. Vigorous experience is necessary, but is incomplete until it is interpreted to give meaning to theory. The intellect is not a disembodied entity. It is found in people with emotions and problems. It needs to be related to every other aspect of life.

The intellectual life survives in a troubled age, not in isolated academic halls alone, but also when made useful.

Chapter VI

EDUCATIONAL WORKCAMPING

An educational workcamp is the best organized form of work period. At its best it represents a brief but all-absorbing experience for the student. It brings about a total immersion in an atmosphere that calls for reorganization of thinking and of values, and a relating of both to practical action. It takes the student out of his normal preoccupations and asks him to relate himself to the total pattern of life of other people who need help.

When is it proper to refer to a period of labor together as a workcamp? The answer depends upon several factors, duration, organization, attitude of participants, intensity of experience. The time allotted may vary from a week end, to a Christmas or Easter holiday, to several weeks or months. It is seldom that a single day can be regarded as a workcamp. A week end of two or more days and nights is better. Several weeks of intensive experience will prove even more educationally useful. Proper organization and favorable attitudes of campers can make shorter time periods fruitful. The determining matter is not so much duration as the experience of absorption into the wholeness of other lives.

Because of this genuine concern for the troubles and growth of other people, an educational workcamp is a valuable instrument of fundamental education. It is the most complete device for serving student and citizen learners simultaneously. When working properly, it is the ideal method for further participation in college fundamental education.

A program of workcamping is also persuasive in winning over faculty members to fundamental education. Many professors, for the first time, catch a glimpse of various academic specialties in relationship to the wholeness of human lives. They see in a specific situation the possibility of utilizing their wisdom to solve problems. Many are willing to consider an invitation to personal involvement because participation (usually in vacations) offers no threat to the established curriculum or to themselves. Even those who do not themselves take part tend to be persuaded. The concreteness of the camp and the project it supports, the clear-cut evidence of educational growth found in student and citizen, all contribute to acceptance of educational growth found in student and citizen and to acceptance of new responsibility for the college.

One professor was an upholder of the tradition of intellectual isolation. He once made the remark, "After all, a student doesn't begin to think until he sits down in front of his typewriter to prepare a paper. And the college's job is to make students think."

After becoming familiar with successes reported from educational workcamps he gradually changed his point of view. He came to understand that one of man's troubles in modern times lies in the fact that so many intelligent persons can think in the presence of a typewriter and not in the presence of a problem or of the people who must face it. After three years of waning opposition to fundamental education he came to recommend workcamp experience for many of his students. He still did not endorse fundamental education completely, but he did accept workcamping as a legitimate enterprise for his college.

An Expanding Idea

To succeed, workcamp activity must be voluntary. The camper chooses to give of himself. His activity is an expression of idealism. He demonstrates an altruism which is muscular and sacrificial, calls for a period of service from his life, and goes beyond the ease of conventional financial giving.

A Definition

In a workcamp, a group of young people under older leadership live among less-privileged folk to offer them the benefit of voluntary labor and understanding friendship. The essence of good educational workcamping is neither work nor camping. It is the willingness to share ways of living, to merge their own with dissimilar streams of learning, for a time.

Young people, boys and girls together, go out to some place of need to work with and live among new friends. They establish themselves in temporary "dormitories," one for the boys, one for the girls, under faculty supervision. These dormitories may be tents or shacks, abandoned buildings, or schools or churches. Campers prepare their own food, do their own laundry, conduct the affairs of their own group, make friends with local people and share labor with them. They take their chances with local food, water, and diseases (with a maximum of health precaution both before and within camp). Students are accepted as friends because of their willingness to live at approximately the same level as local people, because this helps to prove their friendliness. But they are welcomed in the first place because of their willingness to work.

The work to be done is chosen initially by citizens. After they arrive upon the scene, students join in discussion of the jobs to be done—in meetings, in conversations, by correspondence after the camp period has closed. The ultimate purpose is a stimulation of self-help. Though the introduction to friendship be willingness to work, campers should push for cooperative planning and responsibility. In the early stages they may indulge in a lion's share of the work, by way of encouragement to their friends. But they are unsuccessful if thereby they pauperize the initiative of local people.

The college accepts a long-time fundamental educational assignment to help people develop in a given needy situation. It organizes workcamps one year after another to further the local process. It plans to utilize the opportunities there to benefit students from various subject-matter disciplines and from various levels of the academic progression. It identifies the institution's name with the enterprise, provides a place for its support in the institution's budget, seeks to send students and professors for regularly-assigned time periods, and plans to withdraw from any particular enterprise when it becomes apparent that local citizens have become mature enough to continue progress on their own initiative.

The fact that a community enterprise is carried on through successive workcamps has important consequences beyond help to local citizens. There is a growth of good will toward the responsible institution. Favorable attitudes toward the United States develop when American students participate abroad. Newspapers play up the activity. New support for the college and for relations of good will toward other peoples are built up. Returning students and professors become outspoken describers and supporters of their unique adventure. Students and faculty, even those who never participate, take pride in their college's outreach into distant parts, into difficult problems.

A History of Service

Workcamping began as something other than an instrument of education. The original purposes were service and sacrifice in the cause of peace. After the First World War a Swiss Quaker by the name of Pierre Ceresole conceived the idea of binding up the psychological wounds of international misunderstanding by recruiting ex-soldiers to repair some of the physical destruction. Initially he sought and obtained young men from Germany who were willing to return to France to rebuild homes and schools and churches which they or their compatriots had damaged. Later those imbued with a spirit of service from other nations were persuaded to join in the voluntary efforts of physical repair and stimulation toward international understanding.

At first the camps emphasized construction and heavy muscular labor. Because these young people came to the activity of their own free will and because a quiet spirit of religious devotion pervaded the whole enterprise, accumulated bitterness tended to disappear among citizens helped, among those who heard or read about the program, and among the campers themselves. The accent was upon services to those in need, not upon educational outcomes, except as the total amount of understanding and good will increased.

The first workcamps seemed to be only a temporary development at the end of a devastating war. But this form of personal service caught the imagination of many people and the activity continued year after year. The American Friends Service Committee, which for a long time was the chief promoter in the United States, had a precarious existence for a number of years. It managed to continue on a year-by-year basis until it has become a permanent institution. By the time of readjustment which followed the Second World War, workcamping, both domestic and international, had become an accepted part of the American scene. The idea had spread to a number of other religious groups and had been incorporated as one phase of the work of the National Council of Churches and of the World Council of Churches.[1] The accent was still on service, but the type of individual chosen had changed. There was more emphasis upon educational benefit to campers, who tended to be younger than their predecessors of an earlier generation.

Since the end of the Second World War, one section of UNESCO has taken up workcamping as a means of expediting work in fundamental education.[2] The merit of the idea has not been sufficiently explored, due to limited funds. In UNESCO'S hands it remains a small-scale pilot demonstration of possibilities in a few selected localities where the need is great.

The workcamping idea has moved from a major emphasis upon service and sacrifice to an emphasis upon education for students. To realize its possibilities, it needs to move on to an emphasis upon education for both citizen and student. In such a shift, service and sacrifice must not be allowed to die. The normal idealism of youth needs to be given opportunity for expression but should be harnessed and disciplined by intelligent study. In an educative workcamp there develops an integration between altruistic impulses and the self-imposed discipline of the intellect. This growth in students comes about best when camps expedite a project of fundamental education development for citizens. The ongoing need of developing people becomes a measuring rod for student self-discipline.

A new terminology is needed to refer to the workcamp which is educative for citizens, and as a consequence for students. Such an organized activity we shall refer to as a community service camp. The same entity seen from the point of view of a college staff can be mentioned as a student service camp. The first title is the more basic one. Both will be used to designate fully-developed educational workcamps.

Benefit for Citizens

Workcamps have become overpopular in the hands of some religious and service organizations. Because attention has been concentrated too much upon benefit for students, the activity has sometimes become unrestrained "do-goodism." Or, when students have come into a community for the few weeks of a single summer (without reference to events preceding or following their advent), the activity

[1] Ecumenical Work Camps, 110 East 29th St., New York 16, N. Y.
[2] Coordination Committee for International Work Camps UNESCO, 19 Avenue Kleber, Paris 15, France.

has become an unrelated expression of vague good will. In either case, citizens are denied educational urging toward the responsibility of self-help. The activity does not become a community service camp until it is fitted into the long-time needs of citizens. An educational institution should not use this device except as part of a program of fundamental education.

In order to insure benefits to citizens, an educator (with some of his students, if possible) needs to be in contact with citizens prior to the setting up of the camp. Some local organization needs to be active in planning, needs to have adopted a program of improvement which the successive groups of young people will be called upon to expedite, discuss, and modify. When serving the most underdeveloped, the local organization may be made up of more privileged citizens who accept some responsibility for their own disadvantaged. They, in harmony with educator and students, will press for cooperative and responsible organization, as rapidly as possible, among those paralyzed by despair.

The practical necessity of making physical arrangements for the promised camp gives the local organization something specific to do, which starts the benefit of educational growth for them. More is involved than selection of jobs to be done, choosing of housing for students, borrowing of equipment and so on. There are also the responsibilities of interpretation and money-raising. (The educational institution should never pay for capital improvements in a community lest it deny citizens opportunity to grow.)

Each camp is an incident in and expediter of the long-term program of local development. One emphasis, featuring hard physical labor, is often most suitable for beginnings when local initiative is hard to stir. Another emphasis, featuring much visiting in homes, discussing in meetings, and encouragement of friends to work, is more suitable for a later stage. Finally a point is reached when camps should cease for a particular locality; their continuance might jeopardize growth of further initiative. But the process of citizen development in community continues with other contacts between educator and citizen.

Benefit for Student

It is easy for participation in a student service camp to become something separate, quite unassimilated into the rest of the stream of student learning. Participants report the experience as deeply impressive. But it can be seen as something bizarre, so far removed from the normal preoccupations of campus or home life that little learning carries back. Such a separation is likely to occur when a workcamp is conducted by a service-religious organization that does little to relate the intense immersion in the life of another people to school or hometown life.

There are two opportunities for educational assimilation. One is found in the educational institution before and after participation. The other is found in the conduct of the camp itself. When camps are conducted pridefully as an important college function, students build up an on-campus enthusiasm. Many plan their participation for months and years in advance. Some save their money over several summers of work in order to have enough to pay necessary expenses when they do participate. When the activity thus becomes a part of campus tradition, the number of applicants frequently exceeds the number of opportunities, in spite of cost in terms of time and money. When students return to the campus they keep the enthusiasm alive in conversations, in speeches, in further study. Such a tradition within campus life helps to weave the unique experience into the fabric of normal learning even beyond academic utilization in classes.

The second opportunity for educational assimilation in conduct of the camp itself, is often neglected. To some leaders the nobility of the work looms so important that they see no need for pointing out meaning. An intense experience is less likely to become an isolated memory if some attempt is made to relate it to other learnings at the time of occurrence. For maximum educational benefit to the student, time must be spent away from useful labor on such matters as meeting within the group and meeting with citizens to plan and evaluate activity. While it is true that satisfactory perspective can be developed only after the camp is over, that achievement is speeded by discussion pointed toward understanding in the midst of vigorous experience.

Vital learnings are less likely to be achieved at the convenience of an instructor and more likely at a moment of crisis for a learner. When the work has gone wrong, when a major misunderstanding has been encountered, the opportunity for educational growth has arrived. A faculty camp leader will be alert to utilize crises by pressing beyond irritation and frustration to new understanding and new values.

One of the serious problems given much theoretical study in colleges is demographic. Enormous and increasing populations press upon food supply. It is possible to approach the matter through examination of the gloomy predictions of the Malthusian theory. But it is possible also to see the demographic problem in the flesh as did students in a community service camp located in a rural area that teemed with undernourished children. The problem was made poignantly real when a family of six children had two die within one week as a result of malnutrition and related diseases. The other four were threatened by the same fate unless the workcampers persuaded the parents to take the children to a public hospital. The experience of winning over parents who were fatalistically resigned to the death of the rest, the struggle to obtain transportation and proper medical attention, all gave sharp human realism to a problem that is usually a matter of dry statistics.

PROCEDURES

No description of camp procedures could be universally applicable. There is room for variety, depending upon participants, leaders, the people served, the fundamental education project and its stage of development, and the length of time spent in camp.

A "Pure" Democracy

Since participants are in a student service camp because they choose to be there, it is impractical to give orders or to demand labor. As a consequence, the camp works best as an example of a small scale democracy in action. There are masculine and feminine co-directors; sometimes other faculty members also are needed for their special contributions. They operate as more experienced members of the group, not as taskmasters. There are schedules and rules. But these are chosen and enforced by the group as a whole. The directors can set atmosphere and tone and they are expediters of democratic processes. They invite students to accept responsibility and encourage compliance with rationally understood purposes.

The number of students will vary from possibly six to a maximum of twenty. A smaller number than the suggested minimum usually proves uneconomical (though even two or three may have salutary effects upon local citizens). Twenty, in our experience, represents approximately the maximum number for democratic group unity.

Even this number is overly large if there are major differences in standards among campers. Fifteen or sixteen seems preferable. If an educational institution feels that more students than twenty should be accommodated, then the number of camps should be increased.

Typically campers arise at the crack of dawn, preceded by a breakfast crew that begins work in the dark. The daily schedule will include periods for meals and rest, periods for physical work, time for discussions and lectures and devotionals, periods when individuals are "free" to follow their own devices in pursuit of individual needs, recreation activities, and a bed hour. There may be special assignments to hunt up tools or materials, to make contacts with citizen friends, to buy supplies. A weekly schedule will allow some variations for a less strenuous week end, including trips or picnics and possibly attendance at church and acceptance of invitations to be entertained in nearby homes. We do not present a typical daily or weekly schedule since we believe that the experience of working these out in discussion, and modifying them as needed, is important for students as they learn the workings of practical small-scale democracy.[3]

As a part of the learnings of democratic ways, certain assignments and responsibilities rotate throughout the group during the period of residence in a community. Among these are the chairmanship of discussion meetings, leadership of daily devotional periods, assignment on kitchen and clean-up crews and on teams that visit in homes, and service on planning and action committees. Policy for the camp and major activities are selected in the meeting of the whole. There is frequent appointment of committees, both permanent and temporary, to handle special jobs and to report back to the whole group. Thus there is experience both with the town meeting type of democracy and with delegated committee authority.

The purity of the democracy is never absolute, but the student probably here comes closer to the real thing than in any other experience of his young life. Students cannot be turned loose completely to blunder their way toward the responsibility of freedom. The faculty director avoids imposing his authority in heavy-handed veto when student behavior is individually or collectively unwise. Instead,

[3] For a detailed presentation of schedules and other aspects of workcamping, see Willy Begert, *Organizing International Voluntary Work Camps* (Paris: UNESCO), especially Chap. IV.

he appeals to the idealism of individuals or of the group, usually to obtain a favorable response.

Typical Functions

Certain functions or responsibilities must be taken into consideration by every group of students as they struggle to achieve the discipline of collective self-control. The all-too-brief time available in any camp will be utilized more adequately to learn self-discipline if there is some advance awareness of the necessary functions or areas of responsibility.

First is *The maintenance of the group*. Responsibilities include such matters as the setting up of camp at the beginning and the final break up at the end. Then, during the period together, there are planning of meals, cooking and dishwashing, daily clean-up and laundry. Much necessary loyalty to the group, to its welfare and purposes, grows out of working together upon jobs that keep the group active, healthy and purposeful.

Discussion is a necessary part of the life together. Time thus spent often pays off in more efficient work. Heightened morale and greater loyalty to avowed purposes are accepted by the group. Young people, even those who have been friends previously on a campus, frequently find that they need to spend time becoming acquainted with each other again in the new situation. The problem is even more complicated when students from one campus are joined by young people from another college. In any new experience problems must be examined verbally in order to gain the understanding that is essential to education at its best.

Some daily period given over to *religious devotion* is important, because a spirit of devotion is essential. The religious emphasis to which we refer must be broadly defined, nonsectarian, the kind that leaves room for the doubts and defiance of youth and will not violate student intelligence. It is based upon the assumption that all young people have aspirations to discover meaning in their lives, meaning in terms of the good of all men. To aid in the youthful search for purpose that gives significance to the sacrifice they are cheerfully making, a period of fifteen to thirty minutes each day is set aside for whatever religious expression makes sense to them. It is best if no set form is chosen for this part of the day's schedule. Leadership of the event rotates throughout the group. Each student leader chooses the form of devotional that meets his need, asking the others to bear with him. Neither attendance nor leadership is compulsory. Campers are invited to participate in both. One leader will read from the Bible or some other religious writing; another will ask for singing; another will raise questions hoping for an answer; another will call for silent meditation together. The aim is not conversion to any faith but the discovery of the common devotion to the good that ultimately could unite all human beings.

All the functions mentioned need recognition as an important part of the experience. Included also may be periods of visiting in citizens' homes, periods for conduct of classes for citizens, community gatherings, and club meetings for children. Much informal but important activity cannot be scheduled. Certain additional emphases should be kept in mind when planning a student service camp. Time should be allowed for individuals to leave the group to interview people or collect needed information or specimens. Other periods should be available for such research activity as map-making, filing and organizing of data, writing of reports, and the like. The main part of the "deskwork" on research will take place after a return to the campus, but individual students should be able to take some time in camp to collect and organize data without feeling apologetic for shirking some physical labor.

There should be room for individual variety in activity with the full understanding and approval of faculty directors. Each camper must learn to make judicious choices between the times when he goes along with the group activity and the times when he follows his own individual decisions.

TYPICAL PROBLEMS

Within limits a competent educator should welcome problems and conflicts. These offer opportunity for personality growth and adoption of new values, when handled skillfully. The seriousness of many difficulties, which are normal to youth, increases in a student camp situation but the possibility of handling them constructively increases also.

Resentment Against Freedom

The relatively pure democracy is often resented by participant young people. They, like some of their elders, seek to avoid the responsibility that freedom implies. Many of them, for the first time in their lives, find themselves in a situation where they are largely "on their own," must make important collective decisions, and must enforce these decisions upon themselves. Sometimes instead of plunging with joy into a new freedom, they prefer to continue with immature habits of irresponsibility and complaint.

Freedom is frequently misinterpreted by the immature of whatever age, in two mistaken fashions. The first is the idea that the removal of restraint grants a license to the individual to do as he pleases irrespective of the needs of other people or of the group of which he should be a member. According to this interpretation, freedom means individual anarchy. The second is the idea that an individual fulfills his democratic obligation when he sits upon the sidelines to criticize those who take responsibility. Young people, suddenly thrust into a freedom much greater than they have ever experienced before in family or on campus, may react with both mistaken interpretations, to resent the situation even while they enjoy it.

Contradictory attitudes will often appear within a group of students. These are irritating or amusing according to the point of view of the educator. Young people will demand that more decisions on policy or action be turned over to them. They will openly or covertly resent those limitations upon their freedom imposed by the situation in which they work, by local social customs, or by the long-time plans of the project which look toward slow change. At the same time they will complain about the hours spent in meetings. That is, they will sometimes demand responsibility yet refuse to accept the self-discipline that would carry the responsibility.

The experienced educator who has dealt with young people in process of maturing is unworried by such contradictions. He accepts the resentment as an opportunity to interpret processes of change to individuals and to the group. He recognizes, too, that the complaints seldom loom as large as do the satisfactions. Any markedly new experience must have negative as well as positive aspects.

Maintaining of Morale

Despite complaints, the prevailing tone of a well-run student service camp is cheerful and grateful for the experience. But there is always a problem of the maintenance of morale, as there is in any situation where people work together. The problem is more complicated in dealing with volunteer workers where the usual incentives of pay or advancement cannot be employed. Indeed, the idealism which inspires the student to take part in the activity introduces its own list of morale problems.

Most students come into service experience with high hopes of making a significant contribution. Actually such hopes are not unrealistic; the unrealism comes in an overestimation of the amount each individual can contribute in the limited time available. Almost always there is disappointment that the reality of accomplishment is less than the anticipation. Almost always there is conflict between the speed of change which idealistic young people think ought to be possible and the pace which is acceptable to local citizens. As one experienced educational workcamp director stated it, "These young people want to bring in the millennium on earth by Thursday evening because they have another appointment for Friday."

Differing concepts of time and efficiency can make their contributions to slackening morale. When college students are taken to live among the less advantaged, they frequently encounter people who have little compulsion to keep an appointment at a given time, or people whose standards of efficient work are far different from their own. Such contrasting differences are especially to be found when American students take part in a workcamp on foreign soil. The student learns how to keep up his morale by understanding the differences, by accepting the prevailing standard with the cheerful expectation of seeing modification in both the citizen's and in his own point of view. After all, who is to say that men are better off as slaves to schedules and clocks and to Western concepts of efficiency?

In any service camp, for a variety of reasons, there will be periods of letdown in morale, of lost enthusiasm and complaint. When promised tools or materials have failed to arrive on time, when local citizens have not appeared to help on a job as promised, when some misunderstanding has broken the group into conflicting factions, directors must be quick to recommend a substitute activity for the one which cannot be carried forward, must be sensitive to group mood and ready to provide interpretation that throws events into perspective. They look more to long-time prevailing group tone than to temporary mood.

Boy-Girl Relations

It is desirable that both boys and girls be present. But anyone with experience in dealing with young people will recognize immediately, that problems of relationships between the sexes will arise. They become more complicated when young people from more than one cultural and national background are mixed in a single camp.

In general, college educators should look with judicious approval upon romances between male and female students. Marriages which have had their origin on a college campus are statistically more likely to turn out well than some others. But, despite this fact, a community service camp is not recommended as a place to carry on a courtship. The romantic interest is likely to loom larger than the purposes which serve citizen and group. It is unwise to include an engaged couple or one that is "going steady." A married student-couple should be welcome, provided the two are willing to pass beyond the stage of exclusive absorption in each other. As for other student participants, they should agree in advance that their purpose in volunteering for camp experience is other than romantic, that the project of fundamental education they hope to serve is more important than their personal, individual amusement or matrimonial intentions, during the time of their service.

The difficulty and importance of handling boy-girl relationships provides one of the main reasons for a husband-wife team as directors and for a family-type atmosphere. The intricacies of a love-affair are seldom discussed profitably in the whole group of campers. Such matters must be considered in personal conversation with those involved. A wife co-director who is trusted by feminine students can work out many a knotty problem with a girl. A husband co-director can do the same with a boy. And the two can coordinate policy for the benefit of the two students, in husband-to-wife conversations.

No educator should fear or become alarmed at the prospect of romantic difficulties in a service camp. These problems occur in any coeducational endeavor. They can be handled constructively by educators who assume in advance that difficulties will arise, by those who create a group atmosphere of mutual understanding, by those who would utilize difficulties to help students mature in their use of freedom.

Citizen-Student Relations

Whenever a college group lives off-campus, close to citizens, there is room for cross-cultural conflict. Such possibilities exist whether the camp operates in familiar, nearby territory or in some foreign country. The differences are more spectacular and noticeable in an alien setting. A careful educator will call student attention to potential conflict as a contribution to student maturation. Students need to learn that customs and behaviors acceptable to themselves may prove ill-adapted or even insulting to citizens. If a student is to contribute to another person's development, he must respect the latter's standards and beliefs, those which are a part of his dignity.

Several matters of custom can be mentioned. The freely-given caresses exchanged between boys and girls on an American college campus may seem immoral in many communities. Certain types of feminine clothing worn while working may be condemned. In one situation, girls could wear blue jean overalls, but not bright colored (particularly red) slacks or shorts, without arousing serious condemnation. In another situation visits by students in homes were acceptable as long as there were girls or women in the party. Males alone as callers were rejected, especially when wives and children were the only local people to welcome visitors. A major crisis arose in one camp when local citizens discovered that a large kettle loaned to students by school authorities was being used to boil out dish towels. Local standards of sanitation held that laundry should not be processed in the same receptacle as that used for preparation of food. The standards of sanitation held by campers allowed for the double use of the kettle until citizen criticism put a stop to the practice.

The fact that they were in a camp unduly impressed the boys of a group in residence within a foreign community. They celebrated the situation by refraining from shaving for weeks. This undergraduate demonstration of masculine virility carried the wrong implication to citizens. They interpreted the beards as an insult to themselves. They felt the students were acting like guests who come to dinner in dirty and unkempt clothes, thereby telling the hostess they had no respect for her. Several discussions were required to help students understand the criticism and accept their obligation as guests in a country and in a community.

It is better if criticism be more a matter of take than give for students. Campers, and especially the directors, should be sensitive to criticism. After all, they are the strangers in a strange situation; they are the people who are called upon to adapt to local customs. They should keep an attentive ear open for critical comments and be prepared to change their conduct.

Sometimes students resent the "interference" with their freedom that comes from citizen criticism or from pressure to cease some conduct which is completely acceptable to themselves. They may then blame their local friends or, more likely, the faculty directors. Even the raising of questions in discussion will, at times, be interpreted as pressure. Because of this and similar difficulties, it is wise for students to spend time on "public relations," talking with citizens, visiting in homes, entertaining local friends. Frequently time spent in establishing and maintaining an understanding friendship may prove to be more important than the physical labor.

The Parent-Scapegoat

The faculty directors of a camp should expect to be occasional recipients of student criticism and complaint. When problems arise and things go wrong there must be some person who can bear the brunt of student unhappiness. Since student criticism of citizen is unwise, the faculty leader must offer himself as target of complaint. Such a fate is normal for any educator who deals with maturing young people. The tendency is exaggerated in the intensity of a camp atmosphere.

A student service camp that approximates a family pattern can make criticism from young people easy but reduce its importance in a balance of mainly-positive relationships. Students will complain, but will also appreciate the experience and the leadership. Some even will end their time period in camp with unhappy condemnations on their lips, only to become enthusiastic supporters after impressions and memories have had a chance to fall into a perspective.

Faculty directors who can keep a balanced sense of humor can handle most of the problems that typically arise. They know that they can call upon the idealistic good will and good sense of students to modify behavior and attitudes. By creating a family-like atmosphere they give room for free exchange of opinions and for arrival at intelligent collective decisions, even though they may become parent-like scapegoats from time to time. They can anticipate many difficulties by keeping a sensitive ear open for unhappy rumblings from either citizen or student.

In theory, at least, it is possible that the professor-parent-substitute might shift his conduct to become the heavy-handed *paterfamilias*, to send an uncooperative camper home, for example. We have never seen any situation serious enough to warrant such extreme action. A sense of humor and an appeal to the idealism that persuaded the student to volunteer in the first place, seem to suffice for solution of problems.

New Possibilities

Because most orthodox fundamental educators have not perceived community service camps as useful, they have been unable to benefit fully by cooperation with higher education. They have thought of their work as a separate specialty that, at best, looks to universities for training of technical experts. They have not explored the possibility that developing undergraduates might expedite their work with developing citizens. A fitting of student camps into their enterprises would open up entirely new vistas of possibility.

Camps can make an important contribution to development of citizens when they are:

Used in consultation with the fundamental educator who agrees that their services will expedite.

Set up with adequate preparation for students.

Led by competent educators who will utilize situations of misunderstanding to broaden vistas for both student and citizen.

Used in connection with technical experts and other members of fundamental education teams.

Discontinued in any locality when their services will no longer expedite the ongoing program of fundamental development.

Only when a service camp proves educationally beneficial for citizens can it be made educationally sound for students.

Double Complexity, Double Opportunity

Fundamental educators are fearful of using non-expert students in situations of complication and delicacy. The fear is justified, when a workcamp falls short of becoming a community service project. When students have adequate guidance their admitted non-expertness can prove an asset rather than a liaiblity.[4] Specialists in sanitation or literacy, or agriculture, or city planning are often regarded with suspicion by local people. Sometimes students, who offer nothing more than friendship and a cheerful willingness to work, are accepted by the same citizens. Having established their friendly rapport with local people, students can introduce specialists in a favorable light. They can continue to work with them in a mutually helpful relationship. Student campers are not substitutes for the technically trained. They can become expediters who clear the way for these skilled people to work more effectively.

What of the untrained youth who says or does the wrong thing, at the wrong time, to the wrong person? There is greater readiness to forgive mistakes in the young than in their elders who "should know better." We have found that when an error has been pointed out to a well-meaning young person, he is usually most ready to apologize because he is not burdened with the need to appear wise. The freely-given apology is usually accepted by a citizen in a spirit that increases mutual understanding. Thus a mistake can be turned into a successful stimulation of a mutual education process. The naïve youth is watched and guided by faculty members who are aware of the needs for the growth of all.

Lengthening and Strengthening

When student camps are conceived of as expediters of fundamental education, they take on new importance and new forms. The first and most obvious change to be noted is the lengthening of time period. Camps may be lengthened from a few weeks to six months, eight months (a summer plus a college semester), or to the year round. In the longer-period camps, students and professors are freer to come and depart according to individual convenience. Such a lengthened period may become an economic necessity when the project is located in a distant land and travel cost is large. In this case the educator needs to be especially vigilant lest the benefit for his students be forgotten in the single-minded eagerness to educate local citizens.

A pattern for community service camping in distant lands has begun to emerge from experience. A specific site for development is

[4] See *Youth and Fundamental Education* (Paris: UNESCO), especially Chap. III.

chosen in village or city neighborhood. A decision is reached by local citizens to continue operations over a period of several years. The interest of at least two colleges is enlisted, one in a visiting nation (the United States for example), one in a host nation that welcomes help. The two institutions agree to supply students, mixing visitors and host country students to work side by side. The supporting interest of the host government and of such agencies as agricultural extension and public education, or a bureau of community development, is enlisted. A small staff to supervise the operation is employed. Students arrive upon the scene to meet, discuss, and plan and work with local committees of citizens. They stay for a chosen period of time, possibly a summer and a semester. While on the job they carry on all normal workcamp activities, but also take part in language study and independent research under supervision of faculty members. Such a student experience can be supplemented by other intercollege exchanges. Students and faculty can have a semester's or a year's assignment on the campus of the other institution, with a reciprocal recognition of each other's accrediting of academic work.

Ultimately a lengthened program of student activity away from the college can become an organized program of international exchange. In addition to contacts with villagers it can include attendance in classes of another college, visits to museums and concerts and prominent people, high-level conferences on matters cultural or diplomatic, individual study and research on special assignment. Students remain in a group but each has an individual study assignment, carefully planned and supervised.

The worldwide task of fundamental education is extensive enough to be beyond the ability of any present combination of agencies to handle. The active agencies need to enlist cooperators. Collegiate educational institutions are the most obvious potential allies to be recruited. The inclusion of community service camps in programs of fundamental education is the most obvious method by which academicians can be won over to cooperation.

American colleges have an opportunity and responsibility to stimulate their counterpart institutions abroad, to enter the field of fundamental education. In general, non-American universities are less practical, more committed to abstract learnings. Their conversion to education for their own underdeveloped can be speeded by encouragement from American institutions. The setting up of joint camp enterprises in support of fundamental citizen development is one most immediate way for domestic colleges to support the fundamental educator's search for allies.

A Beginning Point

The easiest introduction to fundamental education for a college is found in a program of educative service camping. Camps can be set up to fit into the normal schedule of vacations; preparation and post-use can be fitted into the existing course structure. A few adventurous professors or faculty couples can usually be found ready to volunteer for leadership.

The program, however, should not result in an occasional work-camp organized sporadically in answer to generous impulse. It should result in serious commitment to return again and again to selected localities, where the activity can be coordinated with other organized fundamental education. A longer-time program of citizen development may exist already before campers appear upon the scene; or it may be stimulated into being, partly as a result of their efforts.

Seriously planned service camping becomes one of the major obligations of a college bureau of fundamental education. Commitment to this activity will add some charge to the college budget. This fact may prove a deterrent, may seem to cast some doubt upon the assertion that this device represents the easiest beginning point. The additional budgetary item need not be huge, not as large as a salary for a new professor, for example.

In general, the charge upon the college budget should be limited to overhead costs. These include travel and maintenance of faculty members and wives or husbands who are part of camp, an item to provide aid for less-wealthy students (this amount can often be separately solicited), purchase of a minimum of permanent equipment used year after year, and such incidental costs as postage, photographic equipment, health maintenance and so on.[5] A college having many less-wealthy students may wish to add a regular subsidy to reduce costs for participants, so as to open the experience to all. (In the

[5] Certain matters seem so obvious as to be scarcely worth mentioning. Yet their neglect may injure students and increase costs for the college. 1. Every camper should be vaccinated and inoculated against diseases prevalent in any territory in which a camp is to be located. 2. Every camper should carry, at his own expense, a health, accident, and life insurance policy.

Puerto Rico project several contributors including the Richmond, Indiana, Lions Club, helped defray expenses for less wealthy students.) It is not possible to give a dollars-and-cents estimate of the cost of a program of service camping because of such variable factors as distance of travel, number of trips necessary to set up the program, number of camps, number of students and faculty members involved, and average amount of subsidy for those who need help. A specific estimate becomes possible only when a particular program is outlined. It can be said, however, that those colleges which go into the activity will not find it as burdensome as they might fear.

Two items of cost have been deliberately left out of the listing: faculty salaries and cost of student travel. Faculty members will usually volunteer their vacation time (when they should receive salaries, anyway) as long as camps last no longer than the weeks of a summer. For longer-time periods, a semester or more, such salaries would be added to the budget. When camps are conducted far away, the longer time involved, and greater distance, call for additional employment cost for professors and charges for travel that few students can afford.

Colleges should make their start in educational workcamping with locations not too distant. They can do so without injuring the college's finances. But as their experience moves beyond beginnings they should look to obtaining financial help that would allow operation in far corners of the world.

Not until workcamping becomes community service, not until it is set up to expedite the developmental needs of citizens, is it likely to prove fully educative for participants. Not until colleges realize the possibilities of such informal and volunteer educational devices will their facilities be made completely available to meet human need.

Chapter VII

BEYOND NATIONAL BOUNDARIES

Most college people rightly think of their institutions as contributors to improved international understanding. Their clinging to tradition, however, limits their influence. They could make a fundamental, more positive contribution.

On the Campus

College practice leans heavily upon the assumed universality of inherited great truths and appreciations. Instructors seem to assume that the values they teach (largely upper-class) are humanity-wide. Students will supposedly become sympathetic citizens of the world by mastering the prescribed curriculum. The assumption breaks down because the teaching is poorly adapted to non-Europeans and to underprivileged peoples unresponsive to the tenets of "good taste." The Grand Tradition of the past is scarcely prepared to meet the complexities and harshness of contemporary yearnings for development and struggles for power.

Traditional Studies

When asked to justify their claim to an international universality, colleges point to specific courses or subject-matters. Among these are the arts (featuring composers, writers, and painters from many nations), the social sciences (politics, economics, history, sociology, with contributions and understandings that stretch beyond national boundaries), and especially to foreign languages. Such studies are all valuable and should be continued but in related context. Their major weakness lies in lack of adaptation through experience with people.

Some limitations shared by all these studies may be illustrated by consideration of the foreign language work made compulsory by almost all colleges. The emphasis is upon Western Europe. The student can select among French, German, and Spanish, and sometimes Italian. Dead tongues, Latin and Greek, may be offered, but with diminishing frequency. The languages of Eastern Europe and of the rest of the world are neglected. The neglect is startling in the case of Russian. About one college and university in ten offers this language, whereas in the Soviet Union, English is regarded as a second language to be learned after the mother tongue.[1] In language study, as in other subjects, the accent is upon tradition rather than upon contemporary usefulness. Neither the rival power with which we as a people must compete nor the needs of the underdeveloped millions of humanity becomes a determiner of curriculum.

New Studies

A few new emphases have begun to creep into the curriculum. Among these are culture courses, area courses and new methods in rapid language study. In culture courses, the attempt is made to understand the thinking of another people, as made clear by translators and interpreters more skillful than most college students of a language will ever become. In area courses there is study of a geographic region, its geology and climate, its people and history and social customs, its government and modern life. As a result of wartime experience, new intensive techniques of language study have been developed. These methods have taught a new tongue to learners in much shorter periods of very concentrated attention. The purpose was immediate utility rather than vague cultural appreciation. Men's contemporary needs call for many more bold and imaginative experiments with the teaching of old subject-matters on campuses.

The most needful new emphasis is one that goes beyond cultural background, to experience, to specific contact with another people. Study *about* can never be as educative as experience *with*. An increasing number of students who are to live in the modern world need to enter into alien living enough to be shocked out of the complacent acceptance of their own way of life.[2] The shock consists of the discovery that another people base their lives upon assumptions other

[1] See article "Tongue and Termite," *Newsweek*, March 26, 1956, p. 57.

[2] Some anthropologists refer to the experience as one of "cultural shock." The proposal is to make this enlightening discovery available to undergraduate general students as well as to graduates learning the specialty of anthropology.

than those which the student takes for granted. The shock is made poignant when he concludes that these others live about as well with their assumptions as he does with his own. Therefore there must be merit in both ways of life. While he clings to his own values he makes place in his sympathies for those of another people. By analogy he can be led to conclude that wide varieties of value are accepted all over the world, each with some elements that can invite his admiration. The ultimate achievement of worldwide harmony is not to be found in the dominance of Western Civilization, but in a synthesis of all patterns of value that allows room for variety.

Study Abroad

The increasing popularity of study abroad falls short of experience vital enough to produce the shock of self-discovery. For undergraduates such travel represents a pleasant and privileged tourism. For graduates it represents technical research. Travel is good for Americans, who are much too provincial, but it falls short of enlightenment for them when it offers no more than preoccupation with campus concerns in a foreign setting.

The "Junior Year Abroad" tends to be a modern edition of the Grand Tour for the privileged elite which was found in the nineteenth century. It too often offers a snobbish appreciation of "the finer things of life," for those who can afford such luxuries. Both this year abroad and the shorter "educational tour" are pleasant, but are too superficial to be accepted as important contributions to solution of mankind's plight. Not even the extending of scholarship help to allow poorer students thus to enter the leisure class will make such privileged travel contribute to fundamental understanding.

Study abroad for graduate students is more serious and more promising. Fulbright and other scholarships have made this type of travel possible for purposes of both research and teaching. The limitation lies in confining the effort to campuses abroad or to the interests of the researcher. The traveler, for the most part, has not entered into the life of the people enough to be shocked into examining his own assumptions.

Educational Exchange

Student travel has been far from a one-way flow. Institutions of higher education in the United States have become a Mecca for students from every foreign land. The number enrolled on campuses increases each year. By 1955 and 1956 between thirty and forty thousand were on hand. The overwhelming majority were to be found on university campuses. There they tend to collect in groups of the same language, or religion, or cultural or national background, isolated not only from surrounding citizen life but also from the rest of the student body. They live in a veritable campus ghetto. Only a minority are found in institutions devoted mainly to liberal arts instruction, which are more likely to be located within geographic areas close to characteristic American life.

Some of the foreign student visitors have been undergraduates. They have been accepted sometimes with gratitude for the breath of the bizarre they offer, sometimes with annoyance for the extra burden of adjustment they impose. Few American colleges have attempted to set up an adequate program of educational interpretation for foreign students; they have fitted them into class and dormitory with little help to adapt new learning to the needs of their homeland. As a consequence many of these students have become maladjusted to their own native backgrounds, finding return difficult. Some seek to remain permanently within a privileged America upon whose conveniences they have looked with naïve envy.

A young Austrian in attendance at an American college had a simple solution for the discrepancy between living standards in his war-divided land and those in the United States. "You Americans should do away with all restrictions on immigration to your rich country," said he. "Then all poor people will come here and everyone will become rich."

An African student upon another American campus became deeply enamored of the mechanical contrivances of an industrial nation. He insisted that he must acquire an automobile to be taken back to a native land that does not possess more than fifty miles of paved roads and practically no gasoline stations or mechanics. The automobile became the symbol of privilege for him. Eventually he purchased a decrepit used car, but refused to obtain a driver's license or to take out an insurance policy, refused until irate policemen and bills for crumpled fenders caught up with him. He was "grounded" by police order. And his home relatives had to raise money to pay the costs acquired through accidents. After the catastrophe of the car, his enthusiasm fastened upon an airplane which he proposed to fly back to his homeland. Fortunately the college authorities were able to discourage this adventure early enough to avoid further disaster.

Another student, a girl from a Middle-Eastern nation, was taken on a trip to American factories. She was bored, explaining, "I never expect to work in a factory. Why should I bother to see how one works?" Yet she accepted as her due the factory-produced conveniences to be found in the college dormitory. Will such a student carry back to her own people much more than an appetite for luxury?

A great many students from abroad are graduates or those seeking specialized technical training. For them the problem of interpretation of American life is even more important and difficult. They can easily acquire the specialized skill without understanding the atmosphere of free inquiry and enterprise within which it grew. They can return to native lands, highly competent technicians with little loyalty to freedom, ready to be taken over by any dictatorial leader who comes to power. The university campus ghetto has helped to isolate the technician from the surrounding atmosphere of freedom.

The actual results of advanced study in Western nations has proved disquieting when the matter has been given careful study. John and Ruth H. Useem concluded that Indian students had not been benefited universally. They remark:

A vast majority of the leaders interviewed . . . express a strong preference for having most Indians trained in advanced subjects at home. Although it is recognized that at present this is not feasible in all fields, the hope is commonly voiced that in the future India will be able to carry a larger share of its own needs for advanced education.[3]

They quote an engineer connected with national planning: "We don't need and don't want the most advanced technology merely because it is advanced. Our country must develop in keeping with our traditions."[4]

Some of the dissatisfaction with the educational results among these people can be blamed upon the impatience of a rampant nationalism. To fasten the blame thus is not to solve the difficulty. Such attitudes are the very factors with which this country must deal in an era of great change. The fact that the attitudes are exaggerated

[3] *The Western Educated Man in India* (New York: Dryden Press, 1955), pp. 127–128.
[4] *Op. cit.*, p. 119.

or even mistaken does not mean that they can be dismissed. A competent educator is as much concerned with belief and point of view as with knowledge. Especially is this true upon the international scene.

AN ERA OF COMPETITIVE COEXISTENCE

Any educational institution which would adapt to contemporary need must study the peculiarities of an era of competitive coexistence. American relationships to the Soviet Union (and consequently to all other nations) have developed through three distinct periods within recent history. These are:

The second World War, when we cooperated with the Communists to defeat the Axis Powers.

The period of Cold War, when we maintained an uneasy truce by building up fabulous arrays of armaments and fought minor peripheral wars.

The period of Competitive Coexistence, during which we accept a stalemate of relatively equal armaments and transfer the struggle to a competition for the loyalty of the uncommitted peoples.

The third stage has been developing gradually with the growth of the conviction that open, full-scale war would result in devastating destruction for both sides. It has come to clearer form with the shift of foreign policy of the Soviet Union in post-Stalin governments.

No educational institution devoted to search for, and perpetuation of truth can shift its emphasis with every political wind. But one which would have positive influence on the problems of men and of nations must be aware of the long-time historic trends that guide the future. Especially is this true when the struggle for victory becomes a competition for men's loyalties, depending upon educational skill for an ultimate triumph of ideas.

Top political figures in the United States are aware of the importance granted to education by an era of competitive coexistence. President Eisenhower has called for committment to a five or ten year bipartisan-supported program of aid to underdeveloped peoples. Secretary of State Dulles released a statement prepared by all members of the U. S. Delegation to the United Nations, with the backing of the President:

We believe the United States must counter these Soviet efforts. We can succeed, not by outbidding Communism in sheer amounts of economic aid, but by making newly independent and newly articulate peoples feel that they can best satisfy their wants by becoming and remaining part of the community of free nations.

We welcome more emphasis on economic and educational endeavors, for we have a proven experience in these fields.

We are in a contest in the field of economic development of underdeveloped countries which is bitterly competitive. Defeat in this contest could be as disastrous as defeat in an armaments race.

We could lose this economic contest unless the country as a whole wakes up to all its implications.[5]

Some Implications

What are the implications of the contest? It would be difficult to list all of them. A few can be mentioned that apply to educational institutions.

Educators, like all persons of good will, should welcome an era of competitive coexistence. They should recognize that a struggle of military power could easily go to the wrong side. Might does not make right. But even more important, the cause of freedom will win in the competition if we who represent it have the courage and imagination to live up to our own democratic preachments.

As the Dulles statement indicated, the competition will not be won by outpromising the enemy, nor by proving more generous than he. The competition is for men's loyalties, for the values to which they can give themselves. Men do not yield their souls out of gratitude for gifts. They give loyalty to those ideas which become an essential part of their developing lives. We who represent the cause of freedom will win underdeveloped peoples by offering some of our wealth, by offering our ideas, but more important, by offering ourselves to stimulate their self-help.

An End of Isolation

Another implication is one which the American people will find it hard to accept. We can no longer live to ourselves. Our domestic behavior, as well as that abroad, is of interest to everyone throughout the world. It affects the development of other peoples for good or ill, often in ways we do not intend. We are a world power, whether

[5] On January 11, 1956.

the fact be to our liking or no. We are chief spokesmen for freedom in the Western European tradition. If would-be friends do not learn of the good things we do, we can be sure that our enemies will point out our faults, at length and with embellishments.

As a people we should become more acutely aware that our treatment of our own underprivileged is a matter of deep concern to the underdeveloped people we must win over. These peoples-on-the-march have identified their fate in part with that of American Negroes. Communist propaganda has discovered that this issue is our weakest point, the issue upon which we belie our democratic protestations most consistently. The decision of both a Democratic and a Republican president to desegregate the armed forces was applauded by underdeveloped peoples. So was the decision of the Supreme Court to desegregate public schools. The effort made by certain states to resist this decision, as though the matter were a sectional domestic issue only, has hurt the cause of freedom and aided the cause of international Communism.

Because the decision of the Supreme Court dealt with an educational matter, colleges and universities have a peculiar responsibility. In the cause of international understanding their first obligation is not to set up programs of fundamental education but to open their doors to all without irrelevant discrimination.

Among the factors with which fundamental educators must deal is the news that is blasted to, or leaks through to, developing learners. Educators must deal with the propaganda, friendly and unfriendly, and the attitudes which underdeveloped learners have toward their nation of origin, and its representatives. Their work will be granted a greater chance of success if the domestic behavior of the nation from which they come does not require too much apology.

American education for the foreign-born is better if it is conducted in relationship to development programs abroad. Selected representatives from other lands are better trained in a privileged campus atmosphere if attention is given to eventual return. American professors will do a better job if they have had experience with the kind of less-privileged environment from which students have come and to which they return.

Communist versus Democratic Persuasion

To many American observers it seems as though Communist propaganda is often more successful than the better-financed persuasive efforts of the free West. Why? The reasons are probably multiple. We are not sure, furthermore, of the truth of the statement. Perhaps success measured in short-run terms may prove something other than the loyalty given by people in the long run. Nevertheless, one method used successfully by the Communists can be pointed out. The agents who are sent forth are either underprivileged at the outset or are willing to reduce themselves to the status of the people to be persuaded. This selection of agents stands in sharp contrast to the American reliance upon the highly-trained, who less often are willing to accept the uncomfortable level of living of the underprivileged. The uncommitted underdeveloped tend to look upon the representatives of privilege with defensive suspicion, while they accept agents who are clearly disadvantaged as brothers in suffering and protest.

Americans can counter this advantage, without losing the services of the expert, by utilizing student learners in community service camps.

An additional countering of Communist advantage can be found in utilization of Negroes on fundamental education teams. Either as students or as permanent older educators, their status as representatives of America's underprivileged who believe in freedom takes advantage of enemy propaganda.

Reestablishing the Balance

Most educational institutions which have become active in development programs on the foreign scene, have allowed themselves to contribute to a technical imbalance. Many universities have signed contracts with the Foreign Operations Administration, later the International Cooperation Administration, of the State Department. In doing so they agree to carry on programs of economic or political development in specific countries, utilizing the services of faculty specialists. But they have given little thought to the development of persons, which must be kept in balance with the material improvement.

Such universities are using only a fraction of their strength. They could activate their own general colleges to set up community service camps. These can operate as part of the development teams already active. But smaller institutions need not remain outside of the possibility of team operation. They can gear into ongoing programs of economic development as has Earlham on the Island of Puerto Rico.

The symbiotic cooperation depends more upon the willingness to seek it than upon the hugeness of operation that encompasses every activity under one administrative roof.

The problem is to reestablish the balance of development which has already been overladen on the side of the economic. The balance will be achieved by combining the growth processes of foreign citizens with the learning of Americans, by carrying our learners and experts to the scene of needful development.

The palm of victory in competitive coexistence goes to the side that the underdeveloped of the world freely choose. They will tend to accept the values of those who live among them. They will give loyalty to the freedom they see demonstrated in people's lives.

On the Scene of Development

The Nobility of Work

In most of the nations of earth with less democratic tradition, hard physical labor is looked upon as socially menial. It is reserved for the lower classes and castes. In some, the types of work are hierarchially arranged, the dirtier and harder labor being at the bottom of the social scale (field labor in the hot sun, the collecting of refuse, and so on) while other more pleasant work is reserved for people higher on the scale (domestic work and more skilled occupations). Among a majority of the human race, a higher education is looked upon as a ticket of entry into the leisure class, or at least into white-collar and genteel occupation.

The student service camp upon foreign soil is one of the best quiet demonstrations of the dignity of any honest work. The students come, announced as people in process of obtaining a higher education (therefore among the privileged), yet they prove themselves willing to indulge in the hardest and most menial of labor. Local citizens look on in wonder, refusing at first to join in, then become fellow workers, and finally achieve a wholesome respect for anyone who will give of his energy for the benefit of the community. An increase of both cooperative and individual enterprise is often observed as a consequence.

Probably the effect upon students from the university in the host country is more clear-cut, however. Many have come from an hereditary leisure class; a few may have worked their way up from a lower status to achieve an education that would remove them from labor forever. With such young people it is almost impossible to develop a concept of the nobility of work, unless American students (who are frequently admired) set the pace. The achievement of this concept on the part of future leaders is most imperative if underdeveloped countries are to move toward freedom.

Privileges Come as a Result of Hard Work

Restless humanity will be tempted to take many easy short-cuts to privilege. The Communists promise the expropriation of wealth. Rampant nationalists may promise national independence with the implication that such an achievement will solve all problems. Or individual advantage may be gained by seeking favor with those who have inherited or have seized power. Or national advantage may be gained by blackmailing either Communist or non-Communist nations to make gifts, in the competition for men's loyalties. In any case the concept is new, among most underdeveloped people, that their own progress will come mainly as a result of their own efforts.

Two attitudes need changing: the despair of the lower-class citizen which makes him conclude he cannot help himself; the smugness of the privileged which condemns local cooperative effort before it starts. The philosophic significance of a community improvement project, even though the activity be relatively unimportant, lies in the gradual achievement of a conviction that ordinary people can help themselves. The economic aid brought in from outside will contribute only to further dependence upon largesse unless the conviction of self-help grows in the muscles and thinking of the underprivileged.

All Men Are Potential Friends

The potential friendliness of all men is not a concept which is demonstrated uniquely by Americans. It comes readily as an outgrowth of student service in communities. Young people who volunteer for camps among the underprivileged tend to accept all men and women. One kind of person is not to be dominated over nor another to receive special homage. They are all people.

Out of experience of community service camps grow friendships that continue often for years after; maintained by letter and gift. The more such direct contact experience at grassroots level can spread to all lands, the more rapidly will the era of peace approach. One experience with a single service camp in distant community is good. Two or three or a dozen are even better. The spread of the idea to every land, to citizens and students and universities in each, could give important strength to freedom and to the peace which must be based upon freedom.

Learning is not confined to foreigners in contact with Americans. It is reciprocal. We refrain from listing the specific learnings available to Americans who labor in community service camps. The citizens in the host country could provide a better commentary upon American learning from such contact. This much can be said—that out of a great many such experiences could grow that general understanding of other peoples without which we cannot become successful leaders for democratic change throughout the world.

American undergraduates in service camps can prove to be important ambassadors for freedom. Under adequate guidance, serving at the level of need, they can be an excellent counterpoise to the best agents Communism can offer. Their cheerful indifference to class distinctions, their sympathetic curiosity, their obvious good intentions supply convincing proof of the vigor of freedom. They are convincing less for any specific contribution they make and more for the kind of persons they are. The faults and virtues of American democracy stand on display, but in the best possible light—best because the voluntary motivation is one of generous service. America will make a mistake not to use these ebullient representatives of freedom on the foreign scene.

Who Pays the Bill?

If service camps are to be found in sufficiently large numbers to affect foreign policy, they must be developed by hundreds of colleges. The financial responsibility should not be left to individual institutions alone. The contribution to the cause of international freedom is important enough to warrant large-scale appropriation to make possible large-scale participation.

The student makes some contribution. The recipient nation makes another. The American college has a financial obligation through interest in fundamental education. But there is still a considerable sum necessary.

The seekers after international goodwill could well turn their attention to the obtaining of financial help for such educational ventures. Dollar for dollar, the money spent upon service camps will buy more peace with freedom than many other expenditures.

During the earlier experimental stages, a developing program of fundamental education service camps might be supported by philanthropic foundations. Such private sources of finance would make possible the establishment of the principle that educational policy should be determined by the colleges involved. For educational ventures, control should not be exercised by the financing agency. Later, as the methods become surer and the activity spreads, the responsibility should come to government. Only Congress can appropriate funds in sufficient quantity to make an effective large-scale effort possible. The justification for expenditure of public funds would be the same as that for economic help to those in need. An educational process is recognized as having as much importance as military or material aid. And only through an educational process are the necessary changes in people likely to take place.

Utilizing Democratic Assets

In the competition with Communism, free peoples have several assets which are peculiar to freedom. Among these are: an emphasis upon service; an emphasis upon the value of each individual life; a determination to expand freedom. A democratic people must demonstrate their faith in freedom, which is a faith in people.

Chapter VIII

EVALUATION

Is there proof of the value of college-centered fundamental education? Evaluation of educational outcomes is easier for specific knowledges and skills. There are standardized tests available to prove the efficacy of instruction in school subjects. But when it comes to results in terms of changed personalities and the resultant changed course of human destiny, evaluation can be made only in historical perspective.

There are three groups of learners for whom evaluation might be desirable: students, professors, citizens. From the first, a preliminary evaluation is not too difficult to obtain. The chapter which follows is concerned mainly with results as seen by them.

A statement or self-description of changes in professors is much more difficult to obtain. The learners are less conscious of, or less willing to admit, the fact that they are learners. An outside observer can see that some discover that skill is required to bring profound ideas to meet everyday needs. They become thus skillful because they gain security for themselves through their faith in developing people, in contrast with a security centered solely in specialized fields of scholarly excellence.

Evaluation from citizens is even more difficult to obtain. Measurement or case study of change can easily seem to violate the dignity of insecure learners. But the whole proof of efficacy for fundamental education of every kind rests upon positive results in citizen change. Some evidence of growth can be found in spontaneous comments made, in description by sympathetic observers. But none of these are conclusive. No convincing proof of significance is yet possible. Prior to the Second World War, fundamental education efforts were scattered; many of them were destroyed by the war and its tragic aftermath. Larger-scale efforts have appeared since, but are still inadequate to the need. And the possibility of college responsibility has yet to come into the thinking of most educators. Men's experience with fundamental education is too brief for a definitive statement. The final evaluation will be found in the lives of the children and grandchildren of those now living.

Some inkling of educational value for all learners can be discovered in the reactions of students. The vitality of their learning can be projected as an indication of effect upon both professors and citizens.

CONTRIBUTIONS TO GENERAL EDUCATION

The evaluations which follow are based upon student comments and observers' descriptions. Some comments were verbal, others written. Some were purely spontaneous, others were requested, but in no case was pressure applied to obtain reactions or to credit those that were favorable. Students were asked for their thoughts upon fundamental education experience on campus, during service camp, after graduation. No reward was offered in marks or favor with an instructor; they were free to refuse or to express disapproval if they saw fit.

Emerging Maturity

Any new activity upon a campus is likely to be greeted first by a compound of ignorance, curiosity, hostility, and indifference. Many take the view that they are too busy to "waste time" upon an innovation. Those who are drawn in are excited by novelty. They become aware only belatedly that they have matured as a result of new experience. Wrote a former student three years after graduation:

I'd just like to say that it was just about the most wonderful experience I've ever had—working in the Program for two years. I used to have all sorts of negative comments to make about the Program—but these were of the sort that always arise when a person is in process of changing. I used to get boiling mad—well, you remember—at the patience I was being told I should have with people. It always seemed to me that once people saw a problem and had discussed, several times, ways to solve it, and had even agreed on a way they ought to do, then they should do it, then and there! Well, since then, I have discovered that the what-was-to-me painful process of waiting and mulling over and so on, was just about the most important part of permanent change in people. It takes time for people to think about things—and to change ways of behaving they've had for years. I couldn't understand this business of not telling people what to do! I remember vividly still discussions with you, as to why you hadn't told someone what to do when they asked you. You made me mad. I couldn't see why you wouldn't. I get the point now—if you had told them, then they'd say, well you said to do it such and such a way and they didn't think it ought to be done that way, and then nothing would happen. You'd wait and say "Uh-huh," and "Tell me more," and sooner but usually later the person would come up with his own way and then do it. Oh my! Growing up is painful and especially painful when one is full of ideas about how others should do things without realizing that one is just as slow one's self in changing long-standing habits of social interaction.

Once a student goes out on a community project, he tends quickly to put on a new responsibility. People are no longer abstract names in a textbook; they are human beings with prejudices and possibilities that must be respected. Neither their ideas nor their plans are to be violated by hasty criticism or poorly thought-out recommendations. One young man who "knew" in advance how citizens should decide a controversial issue was silent in meeting after meeting, and expressed only tentative opinions when called upon. He explained to his colleagues and to the professor, "I was afraid I might interfere with the project they have under way. Gee, I didn't want to get us thrown out."

Intellectual Growth

The usual measure of college progress is the academic mark. What effect does participation in fundamental education have upon the gradings which are collected by a registrar's office? Probably very little. As one student remarked: "In this respect this experience will raise the level of college work in its value to me although I do not expect a great increase in marks." [1]

The experiences seem to have intellectual outcomes for college young people supplementary to formally-recorded progress. Or they point to an interrelatedness of meaning. (Usual college marks are awarded for performance in each separate course, not for integration or application thereof.) One student wrote on an evaluative essay: "A workcamp is an excellent supplement to academic labor done in a

[1] All the quotations that follow are excerpted from student letters or essays unless otherwise indicated. A line between the quotations indicates that the comments come from separate individuals.

university or college." Another student of the social sciences wrote upon her comprehensive senior examination:

However, I feel that the most valuable course I have had here has been Community Problems. It has served to give some purpose and meaning to the jumbled facts, theories and attitudes I had previously absorbed. It has brought some organization and direction where previously there was little. It has served to show me practical ways in which to apply what I have spent three years in learning.

It is characteristic of American college education that no grade will be given for a final comprehensive examination, which attempts to persuade the student to organize the "jumble" into some kind of integration. Rather the "grade-point average" upon which he is judged is likely to be a mathematical average. The hoped-for integration is often forgotten because unrewarded.

Illumination of Formal Subject-Matter

Even a short exposure to fundamental education experience convinces most students that their formal learning has taken on a new illumination. After a few weeks in a summer workcamp, evaluative essays contain such comments as the following. The first is from a university student of agriculture:

When I started college I began to pile up in my mind many sorts of different types of facts. When the school year was over it was as full of these facts as a duffel bag is full of Army items! I was so tired of quizzes, tests, laboratory exercises, lectures and assignments that I realized that I needed a mental rest. So I came to workcamp hoping to have that rest and at the same time try to put in order the facts that I had piled up in my mind.

In workcamp I had the opportunity of facing and observing nature. Observing it I could recall and understand better the ideas and facts with which we were sprayed in our Botany lectures and laboratory exercises.

I had the opportunity of working, visiting and talking with different types of people. Doing this I could get acquainted with the facts which we were obliged to memorize in our Sociology and Social Psychology courses. Visiting some farmers I learned several things not covered in Agronomy and Horticulture courses. I understood some of the most common agricultural problems in Puerto Rico. Since I am a student of Agriculture this made me feel more interested in this profession.

But students of other subject-matters were convinced of the application to their special fields:

Speaking more of the educational value of the camp, I have found it the best place where I can get into practice what I have been studying in my home economics classes. Beginning with the camp itself and extending to the valley people, I have been dealing with problems of nutrition, budgeting, clothing, home management, health problems, etc.

It is my opinion that the ones who have received more benefit from this workcamp have been the home economic students because here everything we have studied has been practised.

As a student of the College of Education, this camp has been a valuable educational experience for me. I have learned to observe our own problems and its [their] relationship to the population. It has been like a social laboratory where I put in practice the things that I have learned at the university. I know better now the social, moral, and physical life of our people. Some of our students do not know our country, and they need this kind of experience that will help them a lot. I will remember this camp all my life.

Lest it seem that enthusiasm comes only from those with academic majors in "practical" subjects, consider other comments:

The educational value in an experience of this type is to me equal to a year's study of social sience and works along with what we learned in our college study. There are also many things that you will find here that aren't in books.

As a political science major, this summer has afforded me various opportunities and insights that I consider valuable. I think first among these was the added interest which I received in a project I had begun during the last semester of school.

Because I am, as I have said, an English major, I am greatly interested in the humanistic aspects of life such as emotions, motivation, desire and conflicts. Furthermore, I find myself fascinated by the different means of portraying these characteristics, or in other words by the drama of life. And much of life's drama indeed has been portrayed to me in this workcamp.

I am a student in Biology and my first objective in coming on this workcamp experience was to try to relate my interest in Biology with [to] a social concern. I now realize that there is a great potential for a person in my field, in every aspect of Biology, but the thing that is needed is the will to devote one's self in part or totally to social betterment.

Other instances could be cited where students have carried academic learnings fruitfully into practical community situations and have carried back into the classroom studies the inspiration and enthusiasm of a moving experience. But of even greater importance are other learnings of well-rounded maturity.

A Disciplined Good Will

From a former student comes the following:

It has been, I believe, a mellowing experience for me [referring to his present responsibilities] as I can see how easy it was at Earlham to talk and criticize ideals and how difficult to show the real measure of a man, which is to work in a practical way in the right direction. Your course has been about the biggest help in this job, bigger than any other—this is what I wanted to write you about—because I have been using and considering the philosophy of group work that I learned there a good deal.

And this comes from another student in a service camp:

The important thing to note here is this: an educational institution such as Earlham College or the University of Puerto Rico cannot, because of its nature, provide satisfactorily on its campus or in the classroom curricula certain of these elements of education. Nevertheless they are essential, I believe, to the development of the attitude and skills of leadership toward a real world peace. I say this knowing well the complex political and economic problems that lie behind the words "world peace." We forget too soon, though, that although we may have technical methods, which answer our problems, we have not yet learned how to work with the people who need these techniques. How do you tell someone that he should change his ways of doing a particular thing when he knows that his ancestors have been using the same methods for hundreds of years? A workcamp is an experiment to discover how.

Other students begin to understand that part of the discipline is the willingness to learn from those who are to be helped:

When I first arrived, I looked upon the people as different, ignorant people whom I was there to help. As the seven weeks wore on I realized that I was the one who was ignorant and learning, and that they were not so different from myself as I had thought, but responded with a very friendly attitude. They were the ones who were patient with my ignorance.

Aside from the educational values I gained from my contacts with the people of the valley was the educational value of living in a true democracy. All the trials as well as tribulations I experienced, all the times I realized that I myself as well as others in the group were too immature for true democracy, all the long, long discussions which were necessary in order for everyone to have a say concerning a particular problem. These were necessary I realize, although at the time I may have been very discouraged or impatient.

We came here estimating ourselves as greatly educated people who knew about life and to whom life will be an easy thing based on our knowledge of facts. And we felt that teaching those facts to the people in the valley we could do wonderful things. But as soon as we came in close contact with these simple people here we noticed that they can teach us many things, especially [about] human relations. They made us appreciate real values.

And finally there is this comment from a Puerto Rican youth who began to learn the discipline of physical work:

It is a fact that most Puerto Rican college youth do not care for manual labor. Manual labor is still regarded as degrading, although not admittedly. Most of Puerto Rican youth actually go to the university to be able to get some "easy" or "clean" job, in which there is not much manual labor included. [One wonders how much this comment applies also to college youth in the continental U.S.A.] They ignore the fact that manual labor is essential to a healthy life, that even a sedentary career needs to be supplemented with physical labor. Physical labor leads to a life richer in experiences, to a life more worth while living. This is what Puerto Rican youths can get from here.

Changed Views of People, of Life

If a disciplined good will results in a changed attitude toward one's self, it calls also for new interpretations of other people and one's relationship to them. These others may be either fellow students or citizens with both of whom the student is working in a fundamental educational enterprise.

Also, I have gained a great deal more knowledge in how to get along with people, because to me here in the camp there are many individuals or personalities. And I have had to really make an effort to get along with them. I think that this in itself has been an experience that is both educational and religious.

Workcamp provides also the opportunity to live in a group. To me this aspect of the workcamp is one of the richest educational experiences. In the meetings we carry on every day we have the opportunity to live democratically. And this not only happens in the meetings but through all the day. Living in a group is a sample of living in a democracy, and in a democratic society. A workcamp like this may be the most ideal way of teaching how to live in a democracy.

I have become more aware of the necessity of learning to appreciate individuals and to work with them toward common goals irrespective of personal or cultural differences. My eventual occupation will probably lie in the field of social work. Even with my limited experiences I have come to feel a need for a renewed emphasis within the field. The self-help idea has become increasingly important to me, and to experience two summers of attempting to inculcate this idea in the minds of a group of essentially underprivileged and community-less people has, I am sure, been of immeasurable value.

A changed view of one's self, of others and of life is closely related to the following:

Religious Values-In-Action

The majority of workcampers who participate, leave well furnished homes. They know little of real need. They come from a materially-oriented society. Workcamps, however, are usually located in areas where people want, they know need, hunger and nakedness. This is fortunate for the campers for thus they are exposed to a somewhat different set of values. One might hazard the generalization that most of these people place a higher value on friendship and the like as opposed to getting ahead and competitiveness. The change of emphasis is refreshing as well as educative.

Friendship has also been a rich experience for me here. I have always been conscious of my social standing as opposed to other people that have not so many material things and opportunities. These people who are so poor and yet so friendly have made me realize more strongly that there is that of God in every man. If I can meet people from a different culture and language with friendship it would seem that I was missing so much friendship in my native country where there is no language barrier.

Before coming to the camp I had not a specific religion. I have had the experience of living that man needs part of his day for devotion. Actually we need more religious people in our world, because this will avoid a great deal of trouble between men. This has been one of the big changes in my life. This does not mean that before coming to camp I was a non-religious person, but I forget sometimes that man needs to grow, not only physically, but spiritually too. And this is education.

In fact, the project has a great educational value and has been one of the most important experiences I have ever had. Every student that participates in this project is richly rewarded because he (or she) not only learns but also satisfies his conscience when he see his social and religious tasks fulfilled.

An Emerging Wholeness

Probably no balance of wholeness achieved by a college young person should be regarded as final. But the process of achieving such a philosophy of life can be initiated as a result of vital experiences in college years. The first student quoted below is obviously searching. The later ones begin to find:

My primary purpose for coming to college was not preparation for any specific profession, but rather preparation for living. I agree that without books this is impossible, but with books alone, it is equally impossible.

Education, to me, is not simply a matter of training the mind in intellectual skills or the body in physical skills. It is the whole process by which an individual attains maturity, the ability to see one's self and others in perspective, the recognition of one's relationship to others, to God and to nature. This involves the development of many aspects of the personality; it involves growth through experience, stimulation, training, discipline, etc.

A workcamp experience facilitates one's ability to learn by lending him a more concrete frame of reference upon, into, or from which to place subsequent learning. In essence all of learning is a reorganization of information into a pattern which is comfortable and useful for the individual.

Most young people are prone to expect rapid changes to match their idealistic impatience. Workcamping not only gives these people the actual contact with "live" situations and thereby demonstrates to them that social changes occur slowly, but workcamping activities actually channel a great deal of their impatient energy. Young people frequently discover a balance between reality and idealism when in contact with the situation. This discovery probably occurs more readily when made by them rather than [when] told to them by some older individual.

One final comment on idealism, written by a student in an article for a hometown newspaper, is appropriate.

I'm not going to say I had a wonderful time and I think everyone should go workcamping. There were high moments and some very low ones. It was an experience rich with the opportunity for growth and it was worth while because of the high moments, but it was painful, too.

Growth of Responsibility

One note runs through all the quoted student comments, the conviction that the individual has gone through a vital experience which has lifted him out of the doldrums of routine. Experience in fundamental education, according to participants, awakens students to a new, exciting awareness of human problems and of their responsibility as educated persons to contribute to solution.

An increased respect for the citizens they meet shines through a number of the comments. People who were thought of as less educated or as lower on the scale of privilege are found to be interesting and promising human beings. Those of higher level become real persons. If there be tendency for students to comment critically on citizens, there is tendency also for them to develop admiration. The realistic yet sympathetic identification with changing elders can grant a sense of "belonging" in communities and in a world where rapid change creates vast insecurity among young people.

The going was slow, often discouraging and exasperating, but this perhaps is the greatest lesson a young impatient America has to learn: the true genius of democracy can only be realized through the often agonizing process of group action. The swiftness of decision and action often possible only in a totalitarian society usually negates itself by denying the fullest expression of the individual.

I was full of ideals that seemed impossible to create in our rushing world —and full of despair of ever being able to accomplish them by myself or with others. I think that the first thing I'd want to say is that the experience of working with you, other staff people and citizens gave me *hope*—

hope that a better world of understanding among people can be brought about.

INTRODUCTION TO PROFESSION

Although the purpose of liberal arts undergraduate education is general, it provides also prepreparation for students as they select their lifetime professions. Experience with fundamental education tends to give ethical social direction to that selection. Some young people report they have found a direction for their lives through such service experience.

The evidence for refocused life purpose is found more often in interview conversation or conduct than in written comment. Sometimes the change gives new purpose to an already-chosen profession; young people want to carry skill to the less-privileged. Or the change brings about a selection of a life direction when none had been clear.

Profession as Service

In a success-motivated social order, young people entering their life work too often seek the prominent position and the large salary rather than the place of need. But many are the future social workers, teachers, doctors, nurses, agricultural extension agents who confess that they have seen their obligation in a new light after they have been immersed in community-service activity. Even those entering such careers as law, business, and politics report that they wish to operate in such a way as to serve better the need they have seen.

A popular campus "playboy" entered a course in community development for no good reason that anyone could discern. After spending some time in making wisecracks about the work, he finally accepted an obligation to conduct a choir in a small rural church. He surprised himself by discovering that he took the obligation seriously; he restrained his witticisms, his smoking and drinking, and did a good job. He made himself acceptable to a group of members who would have rejected him under ordinary circumstances. He came to understand and sympathize with their beliefs, which he could not accept. He helped them fit their church into an over-all community improvement project involving all local organizations. As a result he concluded that his assignment in life was "to work with people." He went on to graduate school to pursue this ambition.

A gay-hearted girl found direction. She had been a cheerleader at athletic contests and "pep-rallies," a cheerful, spontaneous extrovert. At a service camp she discovered that her easy-going flow of enthusiasm was often ill-advised, had hurt citizen feelings. When her errors were discussed with her she apologized, thereby increasing her acceptance. As a result of such self-discipline she finally decided that she would enter the teaching field among the underprivileged. She took an assignment with a missionary board in a Middle-Eastern country.

In neither case did the young person lose spontaneity to become a sobersided "do-gooder." Both continued to be cheerful and friendly. But a new purpose for both provided a basis for self-discipline which allowed their virtues of extroversion to prove useful.

For student, for citizen, the purpose of the fundamental educator is not to upset personality or to induce learners to accept another occupation. It is rather to help them make whatever characteristics they possess more valuable to serve all men. Fundamental education emphases can illumine many occupations.

A firm of planning engineers, employed as consultants by one city, utilized student cooperation to carry forward work of survey and discussion of master plan. Said the head of the firm to the professor in charge of fundamental education, "We appreciate very much the opportunity to work with you. We are learning so much from our contact with you." The professor replied, "I thought the shoe was on the other foot. We are learning from you."

"Oh no," said the planning engineer, "I am serious about this. You have been helping us to get the emphasis we lack, the understanding of human beings and of human problems. You see, we planners concentrate upon buildings and streets and physical structures. We need to be made sensitive to the people who are to use the structures, and to their participation in the planning. We are getting that emphasis from you."

A former student, now the executive secretary of a city planning commission, wrote in an evaluative letter:

Students involved are not necessarily going to be professional in the field of public administration. They will follow their own pursuits—scientists, chemists, labor leaders, business leaders, and other skills that are vital to our modern community life. They will be leaders in community development, since they have seen some of the cancerous effect of apathy towards community problems. Not many people are born, educated and developed into "full persons" on the front steps of the State House or in Federal

Buildings. This is done at the local level by whatever tools are available locally. It is a crime that, in many cases, here too is the seed of apathy, dissension and the "let someone else do it" attitude. The Community Dynamics program as it progresses will develop a type of person who can take perspective of community existence, have a cross-section knowledge of the workings of a community and will know how to coordinate and be liaison between citizens and those who are expert in their particular fields and can reduce to plans the roadmap that a particular community wishes to use as a standard of development.

One ex-student who has taken first steps toward a promising career in politics wrote:

As a result of my time in that workcamp, I came to realize that you can be a Christian and yet be intelligently useful at the same time. You showed us that it is possible to be a practical idealist. The world needs more people like that.

A former student working in a housing project in the slum of a large eastern city wrote:

This course was one of the few practical experiences I had in school. I have been out of school five years now and am at the present time working in a community service project. Before this I was working in a similar project in Puerto Rico. It is difficult to look back five years and determine exactly what I gained in my Community Dynamics course to help me today in my practical life work. However, I realize more and more today that this has been a great stimulus for my present interest in community work and no doubt many of the things I do in my work reflect the experience I had in this practical course of study.

Another student is employed in the United Community Services office (a Community Chest coordinating bureau) of a large city. She writes:

While working for three years on social research studies in a private social research organization and one and a half years on research and administrative work in a United Community Services organization, I have become increasingly understanding and appreciative of intangible values inherent in background experience in the Program of Community Dynamics. . . . The extent of success and happiness in individual lives in the complex societies of modern civilization depends largely upon ability to cooperate with others and to stimulate others to cooperate in working toward harmonious group living, from small family groups, to professional and business groups, to community, state, national and international groups.

Therefore this sensitivity to and understanding of personal and inter-personal dynamics which is developed through Community Dynamics, together with knowledge of methods to guide such dynamics for com-munity betterment, and firsthand experience in using these methods which are obtained through this Program, give one invaluable background for any pattern of life one may choose to follow after graduation.

The author of the following comment is employed by a religious organization in another large city.

Community Dynamics has proven to me to be the most useful course I took in college. My job consists of working in one of Philadelphia's bad housing areas and your philosophy and methods have proven invaluable. I found, for example, I couldn't use the vocabulary or share many of the ideas learned in the more technical courses of college very well here but I could use my experience in showing how people can and have worked to-gether to live a more decent life. But more than anything else, I have gained in the Course the faith that people even in the most deplorable conditions can organize themselves in this democratic way for self-im-provement—something the world needs a great deal of.

A former student now a rural minister writes his evaluation:

Because the Program of Community Dynamics boldly wrestles with the basic problem of human relations; because it works on the community level where men can meet each other face to face; because it is centered in a profound faith in the inherent problem-solving abilities of all human beings regardless of color, class, vocation, or social status; because it affords students in human relations a unique opportunity of "learning by doing" in the practical setting of rural, urban, and international com-munities while they are still under the guidance of educators and text-books; I consider the Program of Community Dynamics to be of im-measurable worth to free men looking for lasting peace.

GRADUATE STUDY

Many undergraduate students look upon college work as prepara-tion for more advanced graduate study. Life direction obtained from liberal arts should give meaning to professional study in many fields. When college work includes fundamental education, the influence carries on to various kinds of graduate study. Until some large univer-sity makes this kind of education available to its schools of law, medicine, agriculture, pharmacy, engineering, and so on, the influence must depend upon memory from undergraduate years.

Many Fields

A graduate student writes from law school:

Community Dynamics, in retrospect, is the one thing which impresses others when I attempt to tell them about Earlham. The Earlham Idea sounds impractical until it is put into practice in a concrete example such as Community Dynamics where it can actually be seen working. But the publicity the Program gives Earlham is only a by-product. In this age of the struggle for the minds and hearts of mankind, one of democracy's most important offerings is self-respect. Although individual self-respect is perhaps the ultimate goal, it can only be realized in a community of which the individual is proud. Community Dynamics is one of the few programs which is working primarily with this problem of world society.

A very important point, though, is that those participating need not be selfless altruists. The actual rewards of working in the field are worth far more than the time put into it.

A student at the University of Puerto Rico looks back from the medical school upon her experience in a service camp among the underprivileged:

I am very glad that I met you. You have taught me a lot. I like your way of looking at people. You try to help them live more happily, enjoying and not just enduring other people's company. You try to teach them to live and work together peacefully without friction, if not loving, at least appreciating other people's work and efforts. Your mind and your heart shoot to a very high goal.

I am sure that you have found many obstacles in the carrying out of your plan. Man in himself is the first one, because his nature is not prepared yet to understand and receive what you are trying to tell. But at the same time in man there is something inborn, which makes him seek the best, a drive that makes him seek a higher level. This is true or progress would not be possible. Wars have not been abolished because man is uneasy, he is looking for something and he does not know what it is. His uneasiness is interpreted as hostility and apprehension. He has to get rid of it fighting someone else. The task you have set yourself is to show man a pattern of behavior by which he can live more happily, diverting his energy toward something constructive and at the same time changing his sense of values for better ones. Indeed I am glad I met you.

One student who did her graduate work in fundamental education gives some suggestion for value of such work at an advanced level.

As a graduate student, Community Dynamics provided me with an opportunity to telescope and focus a vast amount of seemingly unrelated material I'd been amassing from every field: sociology, psychology, biology, civics, history, etc. Then it opened an avenue for putting vague theories into practice; for putting them to the acid test of reality with people and problems that could not be manipulated as in a laboratory.

Now that I am a non-professional and just a wife and mother, I do not feel that I am "just a wife and mother." Working with various civic groups addressing problems of mental health, inter-racial integration and housing, I am renewing the faith I gained at Earlham that no problem is so big nor so overwhelming that an enlightened citizenry working together in mutual understanding, cannot solve it.

[Then she adds, slyly], I hope you won't hear the "Hearts and Flowers" behind the statement. For more than ever now I'm realizing how much solid stuff there is to be gained through the Community Dynamics Program.

If the "hearts and flowers" motif seems to loom large in many of the evaluative comments offered by students, there should be no occasion for professorial self-congratulation. The note of gratitude is to be ascribed less to merit on the part of instructors than to the fact that the experience answered some hunger for practical idealism, when young people face the serious business of living in the world.

In the comments given, evaluations stress philosophic purpose more than technical skills of graduate learning. This fact can be attributed partly to the newness of fundamental education experience. In addition, however, students are responding to the element which is missing in most professional training, an understanding of the people the technical skills were meant to serve. If students going on to graduate studies are made alert to human need, if they can give social purpose to the skills they acquire, then they become better professional performers.

Careers in Fundamental Education

The field of professional fundamental education is so new that no generally agreed-upon training is available. Students work within a graduate program in the field or do their work in psychology, sociology, anthropology, in schools of religion, education, planning, and many others. There is no approved road. There is an attitude, a purpose in life that can apply to many fields of professional preparation.

A Student Learns from Life

Joe came to an American campus shortly after the Second World War, a refugee from totalitarian oppression in Europe. Joe was a little older than most American students, but not older than returning GI's. He was old enough to have strong and relatively fixed opinions which he voiced freely and often. Among his enthusiastic hates were these same ex-soldiers. To him they still exhaled a sour odor of military rule.

Joe, together with his family, had escaped from the Nazis several years before we saw him. The family had spent the intervening time knocking about from country to country, but landing finally in English-speaking territory amidst democratic traditions. By the time he reached the campus, he could handle English like a native, including slang. And he knew enough about democratic government and customs to be verbose in criticism.

It was, perhaps, understandable enough that he was bitter and cynical. He was against Americans and their ways of handling affairs, pointing out the painful contrasts between hopes and realizations. The slow processes of change by consent which are essential to democracy aroused his ire. Although he gave loud endorsement to democracy, he seemed to wish to reach that happy state by forcing people to behave as he thought they should. He was a pacifist, but a militant one. Although he would not attack an opponent bodily, he would do coercive injury to his personality by sneering attacks on his beliefs.

Needless to say, Joe was unpopular with his fellow students. They insisted that he was obnoxious even when they agreed with a few of his ideas. Other students disliked and distrusted him because they felt he had no trust in them.

After several semesters of unhappiness on campus, he signed up for the course in Community Problems. He told us later that he came into the course with the avowed purpose of "breaking it up." He was sure that people had to be lined up and disciplined into goodness. Joe made an honest effort to break things up, by attacking, introducing irrelevancies, and arguing interminably. He was met with whatever kindly patience instructors could muster.

The community action upon which he accepted a voluntary assignment was a self-survey conducted by a committee of citizens bent upon improvement. The committee, composed of representatives from a wide variety of organizations, met weekly with students sitting in to help in the planning. Among the citizens was a representative from the American Legion. Here was an antagonist to challenge all of Joe's energetic pacifism. Yet, by this time, Joe wanted to see the survey go through; he wanted to see the citizens succeed in improving their community.

Fortunately, the Legion man was silent and uncommunicative. He required some encouragement to make his contribution in meeting. An instructor spent some time "drawing him out" with question and cheerful comment. Later, Joe was heard describing in detail to a fellow student how "we buttered up the Legionnaire" so that he became an enthusiastic member of the committee.

Joe and other students continued to meet with the community committee each week. After six weeks the instructor was amused to find that Joe and the Legion man were now conversing on a nickname basis. Citizen and student were addressing each other as Bob and Joe and each was deferring to the other for his opinion on important issues. The cooperative relationship continued throughout the project, until the end of the school year and Joe's graduation.

After graduation Joe had confessions to make. Yes, he had tried to make life uncomfortable for the instructor, had sought "to get the professor's goat." He had been impressed by the patience and willingness to let him express himself. He admitted that life had now taken on a more positive color. He now believed in the slower democratic processes. He now accepted the gentler method for encouraging people to grow and change. He now believed in people, in their hidden potentials for good will, even when they differed sharply with his views.

His changed orientation gave him his future occupation. Joe decided to go into research with people, in the social sciences. He went on into graduate work in anthropology at a university, loudly singing the praises of his undergraduate experience with real people in a real community.

Joe's reorientation to life had practical outcomes as well. While in graduate school he began conducting service projects under church auspices (in spite of earlier condemnation of organized religion). After obtaining an advanced degree he went into a life career of work with underdeveloped peoples. He was sent out as a research anthropologist to live among disadvantaged peoples.

Joe's advance from bitterness to patient belief in people and in working democracy is more than a matter of technical training. It is also a matter of change of basic purposes. He is highly-skilled in his field, but his usefulness grows out of philosophic orientation that turns his knowledge to humane use.

Long-Time Evaluation

Evaluation of or by students is indicative, not conclusive. The evidence presented in this chapter is not final for the young people involved. The real proof for them will be found in the outcome of their entire lives. The evidence is only suggestive for co-learning citizens. The course of their entire lives must be given consideration too. Evaluation of any education which is really fundamental must look into the whole of individual development and give consideration to long-time historic trends.

When fundamental educators make a choice of objectives and methods, they indulge in an act of faith. They make a choice before the conclusive evidence is available, before the future can pass judgment. They must make the choice of faith because they are, in part, the molders of the future.

The upholders of freedom cannot remain inactive because they are unable to prove the correctness of the action they advocate. They must have faith, in the future, in the religious values of their tradition, in people, in ethically-guided intelligence.

Chapter IX

OPPORTUNITIES

Mankind's ills will not be cured by education. But they will not be cured without it. Unless there is a strong educational ingredient in whatever remedies are prescribed, the cure will be neither healthy nor permanent. Higher standards of living need to become universal, more productive ways of making a living must be found for millions, health standards and family life need improvement, responsible political participation needs to increase, everywhere. But unless more people appear who are strong enough to carry the burdens of freedom, the other changes will leave men in a worse plight than ever. The production of better people is an educational assignment.

Change and Challenge

Tremendous opportunities lie in an educational program that acknowledges the challenge of an age in ferment. If courageous enough, it can help guide inevitable change toward freedom on a worldwide scale. Such far-reaching influence is possible in an approach that sees human development as a major responsibility, and is addressed to all men whatever their present background or location. The claim is broad. So are the opportunities.

The broadness of this book may leave many a reader dissatisfied. It does not concern itself with fundamental education only, nor with higher education alone. It is not a handbook on adult education nor on community development. It is not about privileged citizens of the United States nor about the underprivileged in foreign nations. Each of these topics is worth several books in its own right. This book touches upon all these matters, satisfying no one who seeks a conclusive treatise upon any separate topic.

One type of human development can occur in colleges where young people are preparing for adult responsibilities. Another type can occur in villages and cities where citizens progress as a result of community improvement. Both can be conceived of as responsibilities for institutions of higher learning. When carried on in an interrelated, mutually-supportive fashion, certain phases of the two are seen to be two facets of the same process. And success in one phase contributes to progress in the other, opens up new possibilities for the other.

The Plight of Modern Youth

The plight of youth in advanced industrial nations like the United States is a matter of great worry to many. Somehow those who deal with youth have failed to bring to their attention the frustrations and the challenge of our age. The excitement of the frontier is no longer available except in the nostalgic form presented in literature and movie. The opportunity to make supreme sacrifices for ideals to be found in all-out war is passing, according to the hopes of practically all intelligent leaders. In place of this excitement, young men are drafted into an army or navy experience which seems largely a matter of boredom and interruption of personal plans. The education offered in high school or college seems tame material that stresses an unexciting culture or preparation for a vocation that must be postponed. Is it surprising that young men and women turn their energy into some excitement, even a pointless kind of their own creating?

Yet these same young people live in a period of history that is filled with opportunities for the adventurous who would pursue humanity-serving ideals. The opportunities cannot be made available to them on their own initiative. The way must be cleared by their elders, government planners, church leaders, controllers of funds devoted to solution of world problems, and educators. For positive effect upon the morale of frustrated youth, it is not necessary that a large-scale program be set up on the magnitude of universal military service. The purpose will be better served if opportunity for significant and exciting activity be incorporated into an educational experience available to all, on a voluntary basis. Even if only a minority participate in the adventure, the fact of availability can change attitudes from frustrated irresponsibility toward a maturity of personal significance.

The Plight of Citizens

Citizens suffer from their own frustrations. All stand in need of that kind of development which comes only from self-planned action addressed to their own self-perceived problems.

A hopeful paradox lies in the fact that the two frustrations can be relieved by mixing them together in a carefully planned program. Under adequate guidance, young people in need of altruistic adventure have much to offer to developing citizens. Citizens who change attitudes from apathy to competence offer new understanding to young people who work with them, about the potentialities of human beings, about the practicality of democracy, about themselves. The two frustrations do not cancel each other; rather the two developments supplement each other.

An Advance that Returns

The combining of human developments in a single program opens opportunity for the return to an ancient purpose of education. Before it was classified for specific age levels and subdivided into intricate specialties, education was expected to produce more competent human beings. It was supposed to develop people adequate to live whatever kind of life faced them. Even the separate liberal arts are but subdivisions of the most important of all, the art of living.

EXPEDITING NEXT STEPS

Relatively little change is necessary to make a college serve the contemporary need for human development. The main change required is one to take place in the attitudes of educators. They must agree to accept new responsibilities, to broaden their concepts of obligation.

Some Basic Principles

No completely outlined course of action can be recommended for a college that takes up fundamental education. Instead certain basic principles can be pointed out as guides for flexibility.

1. No college should undertake fundamental education responsibility without a genuine commitment to the idea—in budget, in personnel.

2. The college should expect to feel its way with its own faculty, organizational structure, institutional point of view, and citizen constituents.

3. No serious community development enterprise should be undertaken unless there is expectation of staying with it over a period of years.

4. The enterprise should be inaugurated with the assumption that the

college's responsibility will diminish as rapidly as local citizens increase their competence to handle their own affairs.

5. There should be an assumption that conflicting factions will be found in every local situation. Part of the educational task is to bring conflict to a conscious level where factions can meet each other, discuss differences and rise to a higher level of cooperation in the midst of conflict.

6. First citizen responses (and many thereafter) are assumed to be immature and even antisocial. Part of the task is to help people find and respond to prosocial motivations within themselves.

7. It should be assumed that certain specific action projects will fail. There will be periods of success and discouragement. The educator holds on through both, realizing that both are incidental to development.

8. Every college will establish certain emphases and methods of operation for itself. It should be prepared, however, to vary the approach with each community unit served.

In addition to its own unique program of fundamental education each school has opportunities that can be classified by type of institution. Many of these call upon colleges to act as institutional coordinators.

State University Opportunities

The opportunity is open for some large university in every state. Two integrative tasks face such an institution—pulling together the bewildering array of its own activities around a fundamental purpose, and obtaining the willing cooperation of other educators and agencies throughout the state. Attention is given to both phases simultaneously. While the university carries on some community projects to benefit its own students and faculty, it encourages every other institution to develop such activities in its own way. Every other university, every smaller college, every teachers college, every junior college can have its own unique place in a jointly-planned program of community development throughout the state.

The public schools should become an important part of any such educational plan. In the United States they represent the single best center for local community improvement, in open country, in the town, and in the neighborhood and city. But, for the most part, public schools will not enter the field of fundamental education unless they are stimulated to do so by leadership from universities.

The opportunity open to a stimulative and integrative university must be met in the spirit of fundamental education. Those institutions that would contribute to human development must themselves learn that such growth can be only encouraged, not forced. Part of the task for the university is to educate collaborating organizations away from education by directives. Such a necessity hurls a basic challenge at the whole university enterprise. Can it reverse some of its contemporary tendencies? Can it cease its endeavor to imitate a corporation administered from the top, and learn to function with more of a fundamental educational philosophy, depending upon enlightened enthusiasm for jointly-planned results?

Land Grant College Opportunity

Unique possibilities open up to Land Grant Colleges (which have become or are becoming universities in their own right). These schools tend to specialize in practical applications of wisdom. The emphasis grew out of initial concern for the problems of agriculture. It developed further with the addition of work in engineering, business, various kinds of extension and continuing education. The commitment to the practical should make easy the acceptance of fundamental education activity that can benefit undergraduates.

Particularly in the work of Agricultural Extension the Land Grant College has an easy entry into and a pattern for service to people in need of development. Too often, however, the Extension Service is satisfied to work with those farmers who are already successful, rather than search out the underprivileged. Too often the Service operates in isolation from other activities of the institution, those that serve business and city-dwellers, those that serve schools and community groups. A beginning approach to utilization of opportunity will be made when coordination of the multitudinous services is attempted by opening up the practical outreaches to undergraduates.

With integrative imagination and experimental courage, these practical-minded universities could set a pattern for many institutions.

Opportunity for Independent Institutions

Large independent universities need not be hampered by state boundaries. Their influence can be national and international. They can set up bureaus of fundamental education that will carry on needed research and offer encouragement to many colleges and public schools that follow their lead.

On the other hand, small independent colleges can often take a role of leadership among larger institutions. Here is a small college located in a mountainous region of underprivileged people. The region covers parts of several states, possessing public universities and land grant colleges. None of these larger schools feels free to evolve a comprehensive educational plan for service to the entire area, because each must operate within state boundaries. The logical coordinative institution is the small independent college which feels a unique responsibility for the entire area. It could call together representatives from all the other schools to work out a cooperative plan of fundamental education. The small school could multiply its own influence by becoming the convenor for cooperative planning.

Opportunity for All

A vast array of potential allies is available to any institution that would coordinate education to serve developing people. Among these are social welfare organizations, chambers of commerce and labor unions, service clubs and farmers organizations, churches, women clubs, and many others. The list is never complete. No college need confine its fundamental education efforts to its own staff. It must, however, inspire these allies to follow a fundamental educational philosophy and method.

Potential allies are available also upon the foreign scene. Various programs of economic aid and technical assistance are operating. Many governments of underdeveloped lands have agencies that press for national improvement. Often the programs of betterment are so new that they are ill-coordinated. And most of them are more effective at the top, national level than upon the local scene. An American institution with coordinative vision will seek to inspire governments and universities abroad to stimulate local community endeavor.

The basic purpose of a fundamental education integrator is to persuade people, institutions, and governments to see their functions in broader humane terms. He starts with his own situation, extends his attention to other colleges, attempts to educate cooperating agencies, carries his philosophy to some other land. He seeks to focus purpose by broadening vision.

EDUCATIONAL COORDINATION

In one rapidly-developing land overseas, a typical difficulty has arisen, the problem of ill-coordinated advance. The people in question are among the most promising examples of successful self-help in the modern world. Within a decade they have stepped out of a colonial status and set up their own elected government, a good one. They have entered upon a long-time program of building, roads, schools, hospitals, hydro-electric and irrigation installations. They have begun to break up baronial landholdings to provide small plots for resettlement of farm families. They have cleared out city slums and built sanitary, low-rental homes in quantities almost large enough to keep up with the new slums that accumulate. They have invited new industries to come in and are training a skilled labor force, with the protection of workman's accident and unemployment insurance and minimum wage. They are building up public schools (controlled from a central office, not locally financed) and a great and forward-looking university.

To give sustenance to this release of constructive energy there has developed an immense array of governmental agencies. These have proliferated to serve specific functions—industrial, agricultural, recreational, and so on. They have arisen as a result of someone's worry about a specific problem or as a result of someone's specific enthusiasm. As a consequence several agencies work separately, and often without mutual communication, upon the same problem. When the public health authorities wished to improve health conditions in one area they found that some twenty different agencies were making some contribution, usually without knowledge of the others' work. Recreation agencies, schools, agricultural extension, local governments, and nongovernmental organizations deal with recreation, each in a separate way. Problems of rural slum versus city slum, housing in both places, jobs on the land and in industry, training of workers to be successful in either place and provision of welfare relief when they are not, all these are divided among a dozen or more separate agencies that can succeed in the long run only when they begin to work together. The planning board, the bureau of the budget, the president of the country, and other thoughtful people are aware of the necessity for coordination if the wonderful beginning achievements are to continue and be incorporated into the lives of the people. But how are separately enthusiastic and often competitive enterprises to learn to work together for the common good?

The problem of ill-coordinated advance is one which is likely to plague every less-developed people which moves rapidly toward a greater fullness of life. The underprivileged are not willing to wait for the slow trial and error processes of free enterprise to bring them the benefits they are convinced can be theirs. They will use their often newly-acquired governmental structure to move directly toward each separate goal of achievement that attracts popular support. When it becomes apparent that related goals sought by unrelated agencies may cancel out benefits to the people, what happens? Governments may be overthrown or a demand for quick results push the people toward dictatorial control. The disparate efforts found in a government that would bring quick benefits to its people must be coordinated if those benefits are to come and become permanent.

There is a method and philosophy of coordination compatible with democratic aspirations. It is a philosophy and method of coordination that grow out of education at its fundamental best.

If educators are to embody this philosophy in action they must themselves get back to first principles. They must make clear to themselves and to others the purposes of education, that it keep service to human development predominant, that the objectives of development be determined by broad religious values acceptable to the learner, that it not rely upon command but instead invite self-development. In original meaning the word "educate" meant to lead out, to draw out, not to impose. At best it is persuasive, not dictatorial. It stimulates initiative for freely-given cooperation based upon understanding.

Educators who hold to this basic philosophy do not necessarily offer themselves as inevitable coordinators. Rather they try to give an outstanding example of their philosophy in action within the institutions where they operate and in spreading the method to the thinking of others. Should a coordinative bureau be located in the university of a country-on-the-march? The idea is valuable enough to deserve experimentation. One advantage of such a move is to be found in the probability that dictatorial control over a multiplicity of governmental agencies will not come as readily from a campus as from the office of the top executive, the planning board, the police, or the military. This is true even when a university falls short of living up to its own basic principles. But there is no way of determining, in advance, the best organizational set-up. Wherever located, the coordinative function should embody an educational philosophy that invites cooperation but does not depend upon the power to command. Universities within developing nations have an opportunity to push for this more democratic method of coordination. American institutions that influence these universities have a challenge to help them understand their opportunity to search out the practical expediting steps.

Perhaps the coordinative opportunities for an educational philosophy are seen a little more clearly in rapidly-developing nations. But they are present also in advanced nations. In them change is also occurring. Wherever governmental authority is used to expedite or control social and economic mutation, the need for a persuasively democratic coordination is present. All humanity faces an era of fundamental change beyond anything ever experienced before in history. To contend with such an era, the strongest of self-governing people are necessary.

The next great educational advance will be made outside of classrooms and school buildings. If it is not made, then democratic man's faith in education has been denied. If it is made, who will take the leadership? Will it be the informal and incidental teachers? Or will it be the most highly trained exponents of higher education? The difficulty and promise of the task should challenge the wisest and the best teachers available.

Educational institutions, by reasserting the values of their humbler beginnings, can become humbler leaders for coordination and guidance of the vast changes that are destined to fall upon the human race everywhere.

The choice of higher education as coordinator of progress is not inevitable. The palm of leadership will go to the institutions which can best utilize communities as educative instruments. The best democratic choice is to be found in colleges and universities, abroad and in the United States. If they do not accept, they will have surrendered the greatest opportunity of the century.

If colleges do not open up fundamental education to undergraduates, then the experience may be limited to specialists in graduate schools. If graduate schools do not take the responsibility either, then noncollege agencies may. These could be churches, philanthropic foundations, governmental bureaus. None of the other agencies will do as effective a job as would be possible if colleges took the coordinative lead.

Overbusy administrators and instructors ask the question: Can the college afford fundamental education? Dare they pass the opportunity to other hands? If institutional purposes are governed solely by next year's budget or the number of probable student registrants, then any leadership for progress is in danger. But if service to mankind's future can guide, then both verbal and financial endorsement will come, in the long run. Men can and will support the educational effort that encourages them to grow.

Not for the Timid

The historian, Arnold Toynbee, comments upon the driving revolutionary forces of our time, as follows: Our century will be remembered in the future, he has written, "not for its horrifying crimes or its astonishing inventions, but because it is the first age since the dawn of history in which mankind dared to believe it practical to make the benefits of civilization available to the whole human race." [1]

Material production will bring some of the benefits. Human development toward freedom will bring the others. Unless the change in people matches the production, unless people mature to control benefits, the blessings of civilization will prove to be devastating curses. The development of people of every kind, everywhere, in an era of major change, is an imperative opportunity that education must not neglect.

Human beings are still participants in H. G. Well's famous "race between education and castastrophe." Another clear-cut victory for catastrophe could mean a wiping out of men and civilization. How much time do men have for education to become effective?

Prophecy is always hazardous, but this much of a prediction can be attempted. Within the second half of the twentieth century distinctly underprivileged citizens must make enough progress to convince them that further progress is possible. In that time period, the citizens of privileged lands must move far enough to become convinced that they can ultimately gain some substantial control over their own fate.

[1] Quoted in an article by Chester Bowles, "Africa," in *Collier's Magazine*, June 10, 1955. Page 40.

Is half a century long enough? The answer depends upon the educators. Taking a suggestion from educational experience in communities, growth toward effective freedom often occurs at astonishingly differential rates of speed. An educator may labor patiently for months or years in some community, without substantial evidence of development. Then suddenly the situation will come to life and local initiative will move progress far beyond his hopes. He becomes aware that people were growing in unspectacular ways during the long period of apparent quiescence. Might not the same combination of delay followed by speed occur in a national or worldwide educational program of human development?

Men cannot find an adequate answer to their hopes unless educators accept a humanity-wide responsibility for stimulating growth toward freedom.

Index

Set in Linotype Electra
Format by Katharine Sitterly
Manufactured by The Haddon Craftsmen, Inc.
Published by HARPER & BROTHERS, New York